OECD Sovereign Borrowing Outlook
2021

OECD

This work is published under the responsibility of the Secretary-General of the OECD. The opinions expressed and arguments employed herein do not necessarily reflect the official views of OECD member countries.

This document, as well as any data and map included herein, are without prejudice to the status of or sovereignty over any territory, to the delimitation of international frontiers and boundaries and to the name of any territory, city or area.

The statistical data for Israel are supplied by and under the responsibility of the relevant Israeli authorities. The use of such data by the OECD is without prejudice to the status of the Golan Heights, East Jerusalem and Israeli settlements in the West Bank under the terms of international law.

Please cite this publication as:
OECD (2021), *OECD Sovereign Borrowing Outlook 2021*, OECD Publishing, Paris, *https://doi.org/10.1787/48828791-en*.

ISBN 978-92-64-72333-7 (print)
ISBN 978-92-64-85239-6 (pdf)

OECD Sovereign Borrowing Outlook
ISSN 2306-0468 (print)
ISSN 2306-0476 (online)

Foreword

This edition of the *OECD Sovereign Borrowing Outlook* reviews continuing developments in response to the COVID-19 pandemic for government borrowing needs, funding conditions and funding strategies in the OECD area. It discusses the implications of the COVID-19 crisis on sovereign refinancing risk, and how to identify, measure and mitigate refinancing risk in light of country experiences. It then examines debt issuance trends for government securities in emerging market and developing economies in recent years, and presents novel insights on the impact of the COVID-19 pandemic on issuance conditions in these economies.

The publication draws mainly on responses received to an annual survey on the borrowing needs of OECD governments circulated by the OECD's Bond Market and Public Debt Management Unit. This includes an update on trends and developments associated with sovereign borrowing requirements, funding strategies, market infrastructure and debt levels from the perspective of public debt managers. The Outlook makes a policy distinction between funding strategy and borrowing requirements. Central government marketable gross borrowing needs, or requirements, are calculated on the basis of budget deficits and redemptions. Funding strategy entails decisions on how borrowing needs are going to be financed using different instruments (e.g. long-term, short-term, nominal, indexed, etc.) and which distribution channels (auctions, tap, syndication, etc.) will be used.

Comments and questions should be addressed to the Bond Markets and Public Debt Management Unit within the Financial Markets Division of the OECD Directorate for Financial and Enterprise Affairs (e-mail: PublicDebt@oecd.org). Find out more about OECD work on bond markets and public debt management online at www.oecd.org/finance/public-debt/.

Acknowledgements

The OECD Sovereign Borrowing Outlook is part of the activities of the OECD Working Party on Public Debt Management, incorporated in the programme of work of the Directorate for Financial and Enterprise Affairs' Bond Markets and Public Debt Management Unit. This Borrowing Outlook was prepared by the OECD Bond Markets and Public Debt Management Unit; Fatos Koc (Head of the Unit), Gary Mills (Statistician), and Caroline Lam (Project assistant). Cristina Casalinho (Debt Management Office, Portugal) contributed Chapter 2, co-authored by Lior David-Pur (Ministry of Finance, Israel). Levent Guntay (Director, Centre for Financial Engineering, Ozyegin University) and Carl M. Magnusson (Policy Analyst, OECD) have provided technical support on global sovereign bond data that used in Chapter 3.

OECD colleagues, Robert Patalano (Acting Head of Division) and Serdar Celik (Acting Head of Division), have provided their feedback to this edition of the publication; Enes Sunel (Economist) to Chapter 1 and 3; Lukasz Rawdanowicz (Senior Economist) to Chapter 1, and; Martin Kessler (Economist) to Chapter 3. Eldridge Katzenbach (Treasury, the United States) provided his valuable feedback to Chapter 1. The following Steering Committee members Teppo Koivisto (Chair; Treasury, Finland); Cristina Casalinho (Debt Management Office, Portugal); Davide Iacovoni (Treasury, Italy); Grahame Johnson (Central Bank, Canada); Rob Nicholl (Office of Financial Management, Australia); Sir Robert Stheeman (Debt Management Office, the United Kingdom); and Tomoya Yamashita (Ministry of Finance, Japan) have provided major contributions to Chapter 1 and Chapter 2. Pamela Duffin (Communications Manager) and Edward Smiley (Publications Officer) have supported the whole team with invaluable publishing guidance and editorial support.

Editorial

More than a year into the COVID-19 pandemic the human and economic tolls have been extraordinary. The crisis saw economic life slow considerably, with sharp contractions in GDP across nations. Considerable countercyclical monetary and fiscal policy responses have since helped many economies to rebound, and largely avoided compounding economic and financial crises onto a global health crisis. Such ambitious interventions were necessary, but did not come without a cost. The 2021 OECD Sovereign Borrowing Outlook explores the impact on sovereign borrowing needs and borrowing conditions.

The pandemic's impact on public finances has been much worse than the 2008-09 financial crisis. OECD governments borrowed USD 18 trillion from the markets in 2020, up 60% compared to the previous year. This is the highest single-year increase in recent history, and nearly double the rise recorded during the 2008 financial crisis. These governments are expected to borrow at slightly above these levels again in 2021.

Despite the large and unexpected expansion in the supply of government securities, the cost of borrowing remained low after the initial stages of the crisis, aided in large part by aggressive policy easing from central banks. Nearly 80% of fixed-rate government bonds were issued with less than 1% yield in 2020 in OECD countries, compared to 37% in 2019, and several government bonds fell deeper into negative territory. As a result of asset purchase programmes, central banks have become the single largest creditor in the majority of OECD countries, holding around 45% of the outstanding government bonds in Japan and Sweden and more than 20% in most EU countries and the United States.

Central bank interventions also helped alleviate funding conditions in emerging market (EM) economies, where the COVID-19 shock initially caused sharp capital flow fluctuations. EM sovereign debt issuance in the market reached USD 3.4 trillion in 2020, 35% higher than the historical average. Debt offerings from middle-income countries enjoyed strong demand, while low-income countries, many with pre-existing high debt levels and shallow local currency bond markets, decreased their already low level of market based funding. The international financial community's efforts, through various facilities including the Debt Service Suspension Initiative, have helped to ease liquidity constraints and prevent a potential debt crisis.

Beyond the immediate impact on funding needs, the legacy of the crisis will cast a long shadow on public finances. The upsurge in debt issuance by governments in the wake of the crisis has increased amount of debt to be repaid or refinanced in the future. Increased borrowing, combined with economic contraction, has pushed debt-to-GDP ratios to record highs in many countries. Central government marketable debt-to-GDP ratio for the OECD area is set to rise by 16 percentage points in 2020 and at least 4 percentage points in 2021.

Looking ahead, the shape of the recovery is uncertain and will likely be uneven, depending not only on the speed of vaccination, but also on the use of monetary and fiscal policy tools – and this uncertainty flows through to the outlook for sovereign borrowing. A number of risk factors could put pressure on sovereign funding conditions, including rising inflation expectations and divergent recoveries between advanced and emerging market economies, which could shift global financial risk appetite.

In this context, greater attention to sovereign refinancing risk is needed, and this Outlook offers guidance and policy recommendations to support the prudent management of public debt under such challenging conditions. Specific measures include the lengthening maturities and smoothing out of concentrations in debt service obligations to limit short-term refinancing risk and limit potential future issuance volatility. Countries that can access market funding would benefit from lengthening debt maturities and building-up contingency buffers through pre-financing programmes. Those with limited or no market access will continue to require official sector grants and loans to ease their financing constraints.

Improving public debt transparency will also be important, and to this end the OECD's newly launched Debt Transparency Initiative will collect, analyse, and report on the debt levels of low-income countries in alignment with the Institute of International Finance's Voluntary Principles on Debt Transparency. The project will shed new light on bilateral lending to low-income countries by providing stakeholders with more comprehensive and accurate public debt data, which will, in turn, help them accurately assess sovereign indebtedness.

Greg Medcraft
Director, OECD Directorate for Financial and Enterprise Affairs

Table of contents

FIGURES

Figures and data available at:
http://www.oecd.org/finance/public-debt/oecdsovereignborrowingoutlook.htm

TABLES

Figures and data available at:
http://www.oecd.org/finance/public-debt/oecdsovereignborrowingoutlook.htm

Follow OECD Publications on:

http://twitter.com/OECD_Pubs

http://www.facebook.com/OECDPublications

http://www.linkedin.com/groups/OECD-Publications-4645871

http://www.youtube.com/oecdilibrary

http://www.oecd.org/oecddirect/

Abbreviations and acronyms

ATM	Average Term-to-Maturity
BCP	Business Continuity Plan
BFS	Benchmark Financing Strategy
BoE	Bank of England
BOJ	Bank of Japan
CDS	Credit Default Swap
CB	Central Bank
COVID	Coronavirus disease (COVID-19)
CUSIP	Committee on Uniform Security Identification Procedures
DMO	Debt Management Office
DSSI	Debt Service Suspension Initiative
ECB	European Central Bank
EME	Emerging Market Economy
EU	European Union
EUR	Euro
FRN	Floating Rate Note
FX	Foreign Exchange
GBP	Great Britain Pound
GBR	Gross Borrowing Requirement
GDP	Gross Domestic Product
GNI	Gross National Income
ICE	Intercontinental Exchange
ILBs	Inflation-Linked Bonds
ISIN	International Securities Identification Number
ISK	Icelandic Krona
LICs	Low Income Countries
MENA	Middle East and North Africa

MOF	Ministry of Finance
NBR	Net Borrowing Requirement
OECD	Organisation for Economic Co-operation and Development
PEPP	Pandemic Emergency Purchase Programme
PSPP	Public Sector Purchase Programme
QE	Quantitative Easing
ROR	Rollover Ratio
SDG	Sustainable Development Goals
SNA	System of National Accounts
UNEP	United Nations Environment Programme
USD	United States Dollar
WP	Working Paper
WPDM	Working Party on Debt Management

Executive summary

Government funding needs and debts, which surged dramatically in 2020 as fiscal deficits increased and economies contracted in the wake COVID-19 crisis, will remain high in 2021

The upsurge in government spending and reduced revenue collection in the wake of the COVID-19 crisis mean that the gross borrowing needs of governments have risen significantly. OECD governments borrowed USD 18 trillion from the markets in 2020, equal to almost 29% of GDP. Compared to 2019, this was 60% more in absolute terms, and 12 percentage points higher relative to GDP. This year's survey results forecast a continuation of this upward movement in 2021, albeit at a slower pace. However, 2021 projections are subject to a high degree of uncertainty largely due to the pace of the pandemic, the global economic outlook and changes in government fiscal policy responses.

The level of outstanding central government marketable debt for the OECD area is expected to increase from USD 47 trillion in 2019 to almost USD 56 trillion in 2020, and to USD 61 trillion by the end of 2021. At the same time, measures to contain the spread of the virus and tackle the health crisis caused extensive short-term economic disruption in the OECD area. In recent months, however, prospects for an eventual path out of the crisis have improved, as vaccination campaigns are under way in several countries. Hence, the OECD estimates that economies will recover gradually in 2021, following the last year's sharp contraction. Against this backdrop, the average level of central government marketable debt-to-GDP ratio for the OECD area is estimated to increase by around 20 percentage points between 2019 and 2021, and reach over 90% of GDP in 2021. However, if large-scale containment measures remain in place and potential additional fiscal policy support needs to be pursued, then, debt-to-GDP ratio may escalate further in 2021.

Interest rates on government securities have declined to record lows, limiting the debt service burden

Despite the upsurge in borrowing amounts in 2020, financing costs of government budget deficits have fallen in the OECD area, thanks to robust investor demand regardless of the significant market disruption in March. Major central bank large-scale asset buying programmes and commitments to keep near-zero repo rates have supported the smooth functioning of financial markets and facilitated the absorption of increased debt issuance. In the euro area, for example, where the European Central Bank has become the largest creditor in several countries, government yields up to the 10-year maturity segment have declined to negative levels for almost all countries.

The low yield environment has made the use of expansionary fiscal policies less costly and more attractive in the fight against the COVID-19 pandemic. The average cost of fixed-rate dollar denominated bond issuance declined from about 2% in 2019 to 0.7% in 2020; and from 0.6% to less than 0.2% for euro denominated bonds. In 2020, more than 20% of the government bonds in OECD area were auctioned at negative yields, the ratio reached 50% for euro area, and 60% for Japan. On average OECD interest spending-to-GDP is estimated to have declined from 2% in 2015 to 1.5% in 2020. Large budget deficits in recent years have led to mounting debt levels, however, the declining size of interest payments has helped to contain the upward pressure on deficits.

Shortened maturities combined with continued large new borrowing needs mean higher rollover ratios and refinancing risk

The share of short-term instruments in central government marketable debt issuance in the OECD area, which averaged 40% in the past five years, increased to 48% in 2020. This has also led to a decline in the average term-to-maturity for the OECD for the first time since the 2008 financial crisis. The bulk of the additional cash needs of governments due to the COVID-19 shock has been financed through T-bill issuance, typically considered as a 'shock absorber' by sovereign issuers. This trend has been mainly driven by two factors. From the demand side, investor demand was particularly higher for shorter-term liquid assets, during the period of heightened uncertainty in the financial markets in the early stages of the outbreak. From the issuer's perspective, short-term instruments have been preferred by sovereigns as the size and duration of financing requirement have also entailed considerable uncertainty.

Notwithstanding the cost advantages attached to short-term borrowings, from a risk management perspective, a heavy and continued reliance on short-term financing combined with rising financing needs can amplify near-term refinancing risk, and weaken fiscal resilience. Hence, roll-over ratios of outstanding central government debt have shown signs of deterioration in many OECD countries over the last year. When conditions improve, rebalancing of debt portfolio maturities should be considered to strengthen the resilience of the debt portfolio against refinancing risk. This may also facilitate a smooth exit from expansionary monetary policies, when policy rates eventually rise in the future.

Prudent debt management will be required as financing needs for debt repayments soar and the outlook for the global economy remains uncertain

The OECD area borrowing outlook has been hampered by unusual uncertainties depending on the evolution of the pandemic and the pace of the economic recoveries. It should be noted that efficacy of COVID-19 vaccinations programmes, as well as the efficacy of the vaccines to new virus variants entails risks. A positive outcome can boost confidence in the near-term and limit the need for additional financing. A strong pick-up in activity and inflation from the Q2 2021 onwards may put pressure on interest rates in the financial markets. On the other hand, the materialisation of downside risks may widen government budget deficits and pose challenges to funding operations in 2021.

The current outlook and increased refinancing needs mean that sovereign issuers should be mindful of risks and maintain flexibility in funding programmes. They should carefully manage changes in borrowing programmes and put additional efforts into communicating the changes in borrowing plans with market participants at a time when there is increased attention to the liquidity condition in the financial markets. It would also be prudent to consider rebuilding the contingency funding tools; increasing the financing capacity through new securities; and, calibrating auction sizes to address imperative challenges.

1 Sovereign borrowing outlook for OECD countries

The year 2020 witnessed a massive increase in sovereign borrowing needs. This was the result of both a surge in government spending and reduced revenue collection due to the COVID-19 crisis. With record-low interest rates reducing the cost of borrowing and robust demand for government securities, sovereign issuers in the OECD area have successfully adapted their issuance strategies to the changing environment and significantly increased debt issuance without undermining the functioning of sovereign bond markets. As sovereigns' financing needs for debt repayments are soaring, persistent global uncertainties call for prudent debt management.

This chapter assesses the impact of the COVID-19 crisis on sovereign borrowing needs and debt issuance for 2020 and 2021. It looks at how sovereign debt management offices have been dealing with the large and unexpected increase in governments' borrowing needs, including adjustments made to borrowing strategies and techniques. In view of continued global uncertainties and higher government refinancing needs, the chapter also provides recommendations to assist policy makers in their efforts to navigate through the crisis.

1.1. Introduction

OECD governments dramatically increased their borrowings from the market during 2020, largely due to financing requirements of government programmes to mitigate the social and economic impact of COVID-19 pandemic. As a result of the increased borrowing needs and the decline in GDP, the public debt burden is set to hit record high levels in several OECD economies. Against this background, this chapter provides estimations for 2020 and projections for 2021 for governments' debt issuance and the outstanding stock of sovereign bonds. In addition to an overview of sovereign debt developments in the OECD area, this chapter also discusses policy considerations for sovereign debt management amid continued global uncertainties and rising government refinancing needs.

Key findings

- OECD governments borrowed USD 18 trillion from the markets in 2020 in response to the COVID-19 pandemic, a USD 6.8 trillion increase compared with the previous year. This is the highest single-year increase in both absolute and relative terms in recent history, including responses to the 2008 financial crisis. In 2021, subject to a high degree of uncertainty, government borrowing is projected to rise further to USD 19 trillion.

- The combined impact of increased government expenditure and economic contraction has pushed debt-to-GDP ratios to record highs in many countries. The central government marketable debt-to-GDP ratio for the OECD area is set to rise by 16 percentage points in 2020 and at least 4 percentage points in 2021.

- While there has been a large and unexpected expansion in the supply of government securities, yields on these securities have declined to record lows, despite the significant market disruption in March 2020. Swift action by central banks has supported the smooth functioning of financial markets and facilitated the absorption of increased debt issuance. In addition, the general flight to safety and subdued inflation outlook have contributed to very low borrowing rates in major advanced economies.

- Many sovereign issuers have adapted their financing operations in response to rising borrowing needs and the challenges heightened uncertainty presents for cash flow forecasting and price discovery at auctions due. Existing mechanisms to market have intensified (e.g. the size and number of auctions has increased). In some cases, governments have also expanded the use of syndications, private placements and supplementary non-competitive auctions to gain additional flexibility in respect to financing programmes.

- A significant share of pandemic-related government expenditure has been financed by short-term debt in major advanced economies. The average term-to-maturity ratios, which had been trending upwards until 2019, fell in 2020. After a cumulative increase of 1.7 years since the 2008 financial crisis, the average term-to-maturity for the OECD area has declined slightly from 7.9 years to 7.7 years in the past year.

- Increased borrowing has also created scope for introducing both new maturity lines and new securities. Importantly, green bonds have become more common with debut issuance by Germany, Hungary and Sweden in 2020.

- Despite low interest expenditure, elevated debt servicing levels combined with continued large new borrowing needs have resulted in higher rollover ratios and refinancing risk for many sovereigns in the OECD area. As of December 2020 about one quarter of total marketable debt will mature within one year.

- In view of the uncertain global outlook and increased refinancing needs, sovereign issuers may consider rebuilding contingency funding tools; increasing financing capacity through new securities; and, calibrating auction sizes. It would also be prudent, particularly for governments that have significantly increased short-term borrowing, to target rebalancing their financing towards longer-dated tenors.

1.2. Sovereign borrowing hit a record high in 2020 and is projected to continue rising in 2021

The unprecedented impact of the COVID-19 crisis on economies and the ensuing fiscal response resulted in dramatic changes both in the size and pace of government borrowing requirements. The impact on government borrowing needs varies significantly across countries depending on the scale and types of fiscal policy measures put in place. In 2020, gross borrowings of OECD governments from the markets surged to a record high of USD 18 trillion (Figure 1.1). This is the highest increase recorded in a single year and nearly double the rise recorded during the 2008 financial crisis (Figure 1.2). Government borrowing is projected to increase at a slower pace in 2021, largely due to a lower expected increase in budget deficits. As of January 2021, gross funding requirements for 2021 are projected to reach USD 19.1 trillion. This amount reflects the issuance needs of government securities for both financing central government budget deficits (i.e. net borrowing requirements) and refinancing debt repayments due in the year.

Figure 1.1. Fiscal and borrowing outlook in OECD countries, 2007-2021

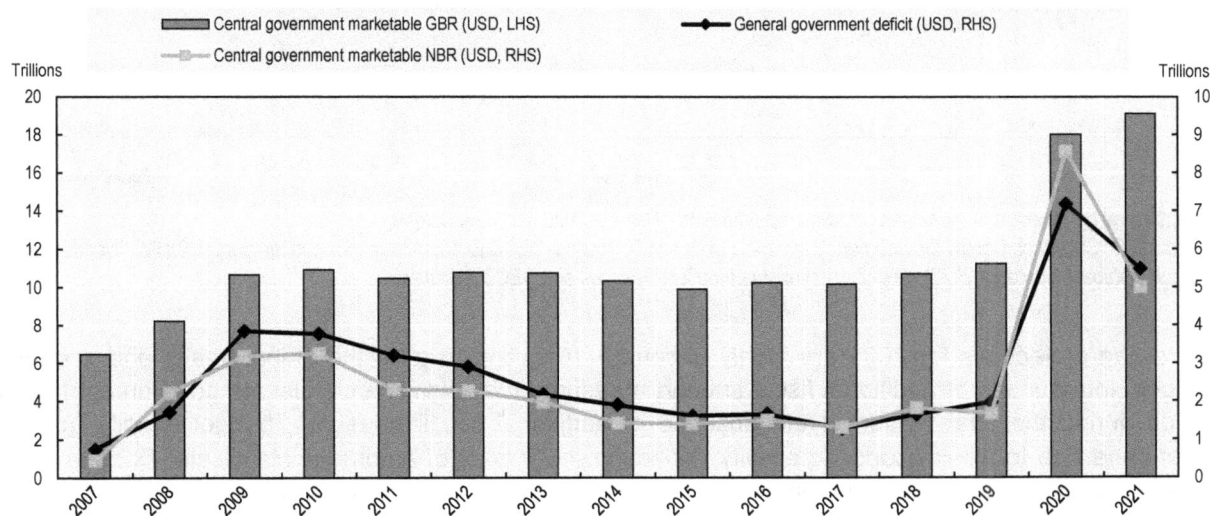

Notes: GBR = standardised gross borrowing requirement, NBR = net borrowing requirement.
Source: 2020 Survey on Central Government Marketable Debt and Borrowing; OECD Economic Outlook (December 2020); IMF World Economic Outlook Database (October 2020); Refinitiv, national authorities' websites and OECD calculations.

Having risen significantly in the wake of 2008 financial crisis, gross borrowing requirements in the OECD area plateaued at around USD 10.5 trillion between 2010 and 2019. During this period, while the financing amount to repay debt redemptions made up around 80% of the total gross borrowings, net borrowing requirements stabilised at around USD 2 trillion. Before the pandemic hit, OECD governments were projected to raise around USD 12 trillion from the market in 2020 (Figure 1.2), the bulk of which again was required to refinance existing debt. Since OECD governments extensively used fiscal policy tools to mitigate the detrimental impact of the COVID-19 crisis on societies and economies, fiscal deficits surged. Consequently, net borrowing requirements increased dramatically from USD 1.7 trillion in 2019 to USD 8.6 trillion in 2020, making up almost half of the total funding for 2020.[1] As a comparison, this is more than the cumulative net borrowing over the past five years, and more than four times higher than the pre-COVID estimate for 2020. In 2021, net borrowing requirements are projected to moderate somewhat to USD 5 trillion, albeit still above historical averages. At the same time, financing requirements to repay debt redemptions are projected to increase by more than 15% from 2020 to 2021, largely due to increased issuance of new government securities in 2020.

Figure 1.2. Changes in gross borrowing requirements

Panel A: Comparison of pre- and post-COVID estimates for 2020 (USD)

Panel B: Impact of 2008 financial crisis vs COVID-19 shock on borrowing needs (as percentage of GDP)

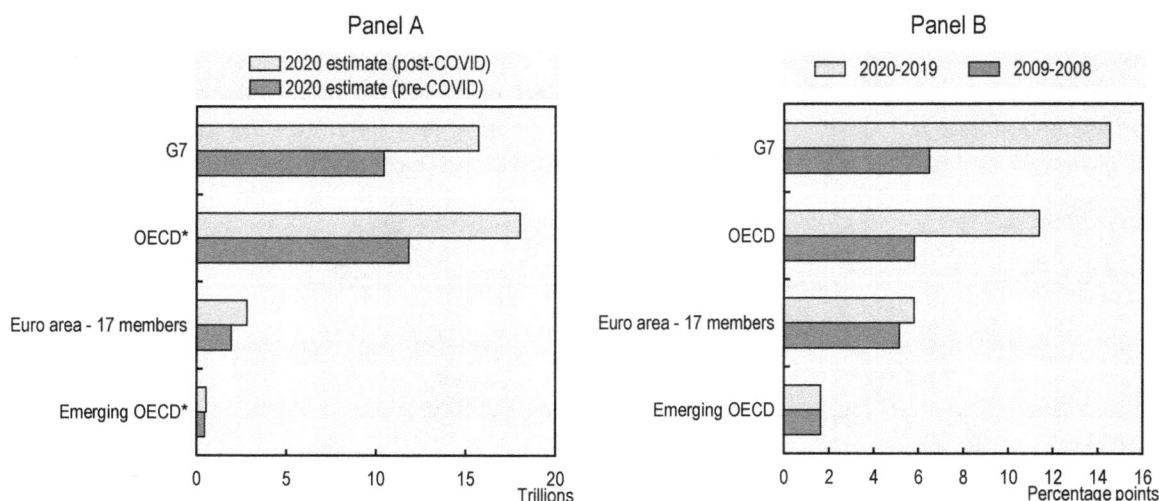

Note: Central government marketable borrowing requirements, *Panel A 2020 excludes Colombia.
Source: 2020 Survey on Central Government Marketable Debt and Borrowing; OECD Economic Outlook (December 2020); IMF World Economic Outlook Database (October 2020); Refinitiv, national authorities' websites and OECD calculations.

Borrowing projections for 2021 are highly uncertain, reflecting risks to the global health and economic outlook. Introduction of additional fiscal support measures may significantly elevate government funding needs during the year.[2] Even in the absence of additional fiscal measures, budget deficits may still deteriorate due to weak economic activity, reflecting the impact of automatic stabilisers. Despite recent optimism inspired by the development of vaccines, delays to vaccination rollout and difficulties in controlling new variants of the virus could increase healthcare spending on top of the likelihood of renewed lockdowns and weakened economic activity, with negative implications for public finances.

Figure 1.3 illustrates the trends in sovereign borrowing in the OECD area. Gross borrowing requirements in relation to GDP jumped more than 10 percentage points from around 17% of GDP in 2019 to 28.5% of GDP in 2020, as a result of the combined effect of the rise in fiscal deficits and the fall in GDP. Since economic growth is expected to pick up across the OECD area in 2021, gross borrowing requirements as a percentage of GDP is projected to remain at around 2020 levels.

Figure 1.3. Gross borrowing through marketable debt as a percentage of GDP

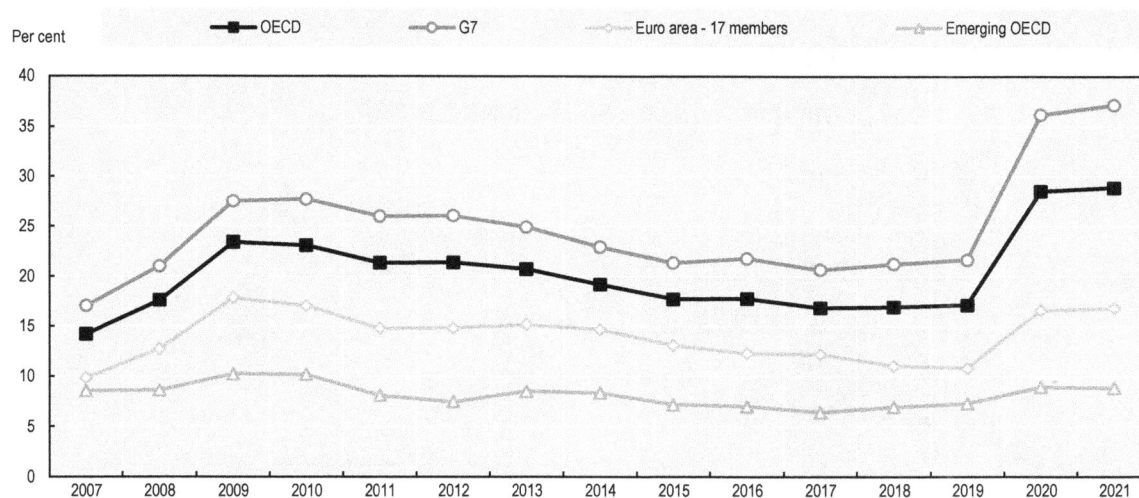

Note: Standardised gross borrowing requirement.
Source: 2020 Survey on Central Government Marketable Debt and Borrowing; OECD Economic Outlook (December 2020); IMF World Economic Outlook Database (October 2020); Refinitiv, national authorities' websites and OECD calculations.

Despite strong monetary and fiscal policy support, the impact of the pandemic on economies has been substantial. The OECD economy is estimated to have contracted significantly in 2020.[3] Measures to contain the spread of the virus and tackle the health crisis caused extensive short-term economic disruption, compounded by falling confidence and tighter financial conditions. In recent months, however, prospects for an eventual overcoming of the crisis have improved, as vaccination campaigns have started in several countries. The OECD area is projected to grow by around 3.3% in 2021 (OECD, 2020[1]). However, it should be noted that economic recovery will vary significantly across OECD countries depending not only on their ability to contain renewed outbreaks, but also on the use of fiscal support. The OECD Economic Outlook of December 2020 emphasises the importance of effective use of fiscal support for creating economic growth by investing in essential goods and services such as education, health as well as physical and digital infrastructure.

The impact of the COVID-19 crisis at the country and regional levels is highly heterogeneous, with significant implications for government funding needs. Figure 1.4 illustrates that impact of the COVID-19 crisis on primary balances and sovereign financing needs across countries.[4] In 2020, the aggregate OECD primary deficit in relation to GDP increased by 8.5 percentage points to almost 10% of GDP. The ratios were more than 10% in Australia, Canada, Iceland, Japan, the United Kingdom and the United States. In terms of net funding amounts Canada, Japan, New Zealand, the United Kingdom and the United States saw the highest percentage point increases. Furthermore, new borrowing needs turned positive in 2020 in a number countries, including Austria, Denmark, New Zealand, Sweden and the Netherlands, which were running primary surplus before the COVID-19 shock. Estonia, for example, re-entered the bond market after an 18-year absence.

Figure 1.4. Impact of the COVID-19 shock on primary balance and net borrowing requirements in selected OECD countries

Panel A: Primary balances in relation to GDP

Panel B: Changes in central government marketable NBRs in relation to GDP

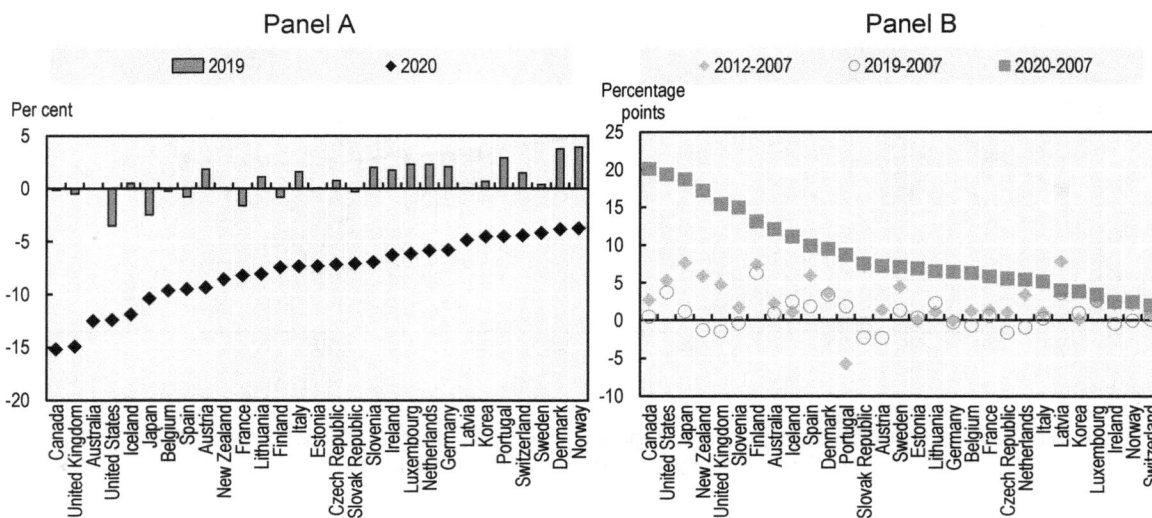

Source: 2020 Survey on Central Government Marketable Debt and Borrowing; OECD Economic Outlook (December 2020); IMF World Economic Outlook Database (October 2020); Refinitiv, national authorities' websites and OECD calculations.

1.3. Key features of sovereign borrowing during the COVID-19 crisis

Choice of borrowing instruments and methods is central to sovereign debt management.[5] In normal times, policy makers consider various factors including medium and long-term costs and risks associated with a wide range of securities along with market demand in order to structure their annual borrowing strategy. Times of crisis such as the COVID-19 pandemic, however, risk provoking a mismatch between the timing and scale of government funding needs and market demand. Under such conditions, market demands for duration as well as liquidity conditions become more important factors in the choice of borrowing methods and instruments than those of associated long-term costs and risk considerations. Sovereign issuers are therefore expected to adjust their short-term borrowing strategies, giving priority to financing the increased borrowing needs of governments without putting extra pressure to the financial markets.

As the COVID-19 crisis evolved throughout 2020, sovereign debt managers had to adjust different aspects of their borrowing operations. In the initial phase of the crisis, market liquidity suddenly evaporated as uncertainty about the impact of the shock on economic activity increased, and investors became highly risk-averse. At the same time, cash forecasting became difficult as government health expenses and, in some countries direct transfers, rose while revenues suddenly dropped. Depending on the impact of the crisis on short-term cash needs as well as on market conditions, governments relied on contingency funding tools such as issuance of Treasury-Bills and use of available liquidity buffers.

While policy measures taken by major central banks improved liquidity conditions in the markets rapidly, the unprecedented increase in annual borrowing needs and continuing macroeconomic uncertainties have changed the annual sovereign borrowing plans in all OECD countries. These changes include increased issuance of new types of securities, including short-term securities, and modifications to the size and number of auctions as well as use of other means of borrowings. At the same time, interest rates on government securities declined in line with robust market demand supported by central bank bond buying programmes. Overall, the increased supply of government securities in the wake of COVID-19 crisis has been well received by market participants. OECD area sovereign debt managers reported that the market remained resilient in the face of the unprecedented size of sovereign financing programmes.

1.3.1. New debt has been issued at lower costs

Despite the surge in borrowing needs in 2020, financing costs have continued to fall in the OECD area with the exception of a few countries including Hungary and Turkey. Borrowing conditions at favourable interest rates were stable throughout the year, apart from the significant market disruption in March 2020. As a result, the use of expansionary fiscal policies has become less costly and more attractive.

Over the year to December 2020, yields on both 2-year and 10-year benchmark bonds dropped by around 0.5 percentage point on average (Figure 1.5). The 10-year US treasury was at 0.9% in December 2020, half of the yield a year before.[6] Despite significant decline in yields across all maturities between 2019 and 2020, US Treasury yields have remained among the few advanced economy bonds still holding above zero percent. Similarly, UK 10-year government bonds paid under 0.5%, which is less than half of the December 2019 rate. In the euro area, where the European Central Bank and the European Commission have been actively supporting member states with various measures and financial support packages, government yields up to the 10-year maturity segment have fallen to negative levels in almost all countries. This means that cost pressure on sovereign borrowings has lessened considerably.

Figure 1.5. Change in benchmark yields between December 2019 and December 2020

Panel A: Change in 2-year benchmark yields.

Panel B: Change in 10-year benchmark yields.

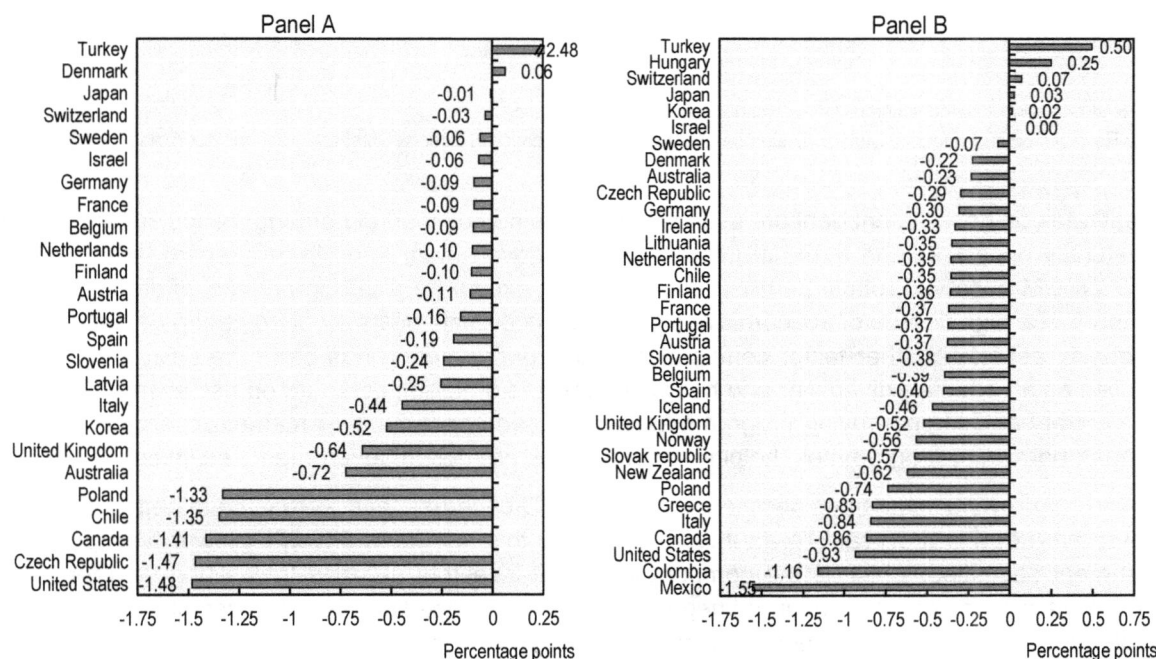

Note: Difference in average yields in December of each year.
Source: Refinitiv.

As a result of this low yield environment, governments borrowed from the markets at very low costs in 2020. Figure 1.6 illustrates volume shares of fixed-rate bond issuance by yield category for 2019 and 2020. Compared to 2019, major changes took place in Canada, Italy, the United Kingdom and the United States, where the cost of borrowing across the maturities has declined significantly. In the OECD area, nearly 80% of the fixed-rate government bonds were issued with less than 1% yield in 2020, compared to 37% in 2019. More government bonds fell deeper into negative territory. In 2020, more than 20% of the fixed-rate bonds was allocated in the primary market at negative rates. This ratio is over 50% in the euro area and 60% in Japan.[7]

Figure 1.6. Volume share of fixed-rate bond issuance by yield category

Panel A: 2019; Panel B: 2020

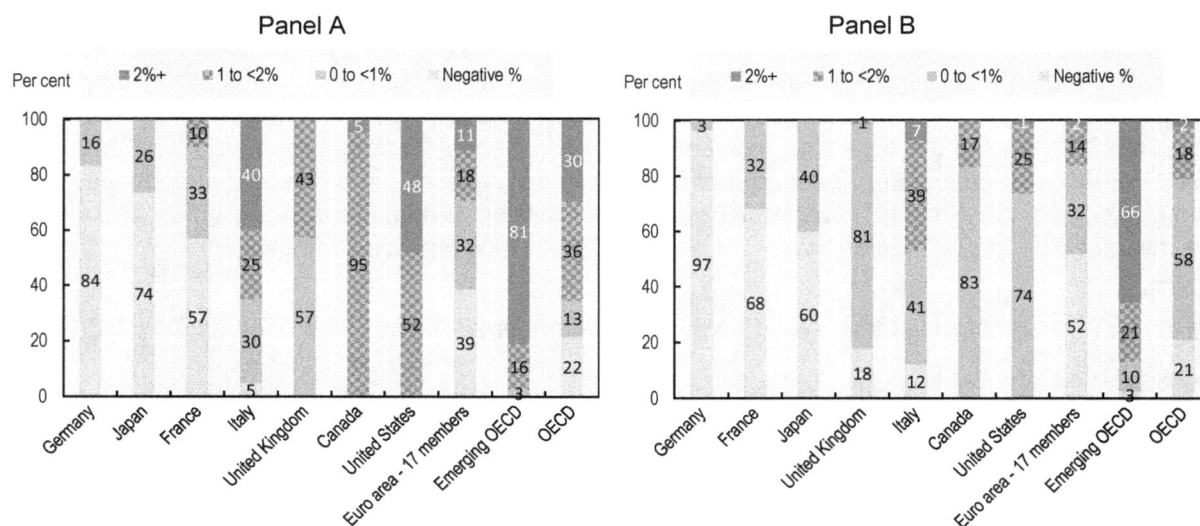

Note: Fixed-rate bond issuances and re-opens categorised by yield at issuance.
Source: Refinitiv; OECD Economic Outlook (December 2020); IMF World Economic Outlook Database (October 2020); and OECD calculations.

Interest rates on government debt are essentially determined by market demand, hence sovereign issuers are naturally price takers in terms of interest paid on government debt. In this regard, members of the OECD WPDM observed robust demand from investors except for a temporary lack of demand in March and April.[8] The high degree of economic and financial uncertainty has supported strong demand for liquid, high-quality assets. Another factor contributing to this phenomenon has been the utility of government securities as an effective diversifier and hedge against major selling pressure on risk assets. At the same time, central banks' bond buying programmes have eased concerns over market absorption capacity of expanded borrowing programmes, helping to reduce risk premia on government securities.

Long-term borrowing costs have declined in many OECD countries, and were even in negative territory in the euro area during the year. To an important extent, this has been driven by lower term premium on government securities, which is the compensation that investors demand for holding long-term bonds. Term premia have fallen or even turned negative in major advanced markets. Persistently low inflation and expectations that major central banks will maintain their very accommodative central banks adapted yield curve targeting monetary policy stances for an extended period of time appear to be major factors in keeping term premia low since the 2008 financial crisis. In addition to interest rate easing, QE programmes that were tailored to target the longer-end of the yield curve play a larger role in reducing the term premia.

Major central banks' large-scale asset buying programmes and commitments to keep near-zero repo rates in some areas have supported the smooth functioning of financial markets and facilitated the absorption of increased debt issuance since the outbreak of the crisis. Central banks in 28 OECD countries purchased government bonds in 2020 with more than half of the net purchases occurring during the period between March and May. Total net purchases by major central banks reached USD 4.5 trillion in 2020, more than half of the new securities (i.e. excluding securities issued to roll over existing debt) issued by OECD sovereigns in the year (Figure 1.7). As a result of increased net purchases, central banks have become the single largest creditor in the majority of OECD countries holding around 45% of the outstanding stock in Japan and Sweden, more than 20% in most of the EU countries and the United States (OECD, 2020[2]). Looking ahead, one risk is that as economies improve, this may generate inflation and central banks may begin to scale back the degree of accommodation, in particular the tapering of bond purchases. This could happen at the same time as sovereign DMOs term out their debt issuance.

Figure 1.7. Central banks purchases and change in policy rates

Panel A: Net purchases of government securities by major central banks (USD)

Panel B: Change in policy interest rates from 2012 through to 2020

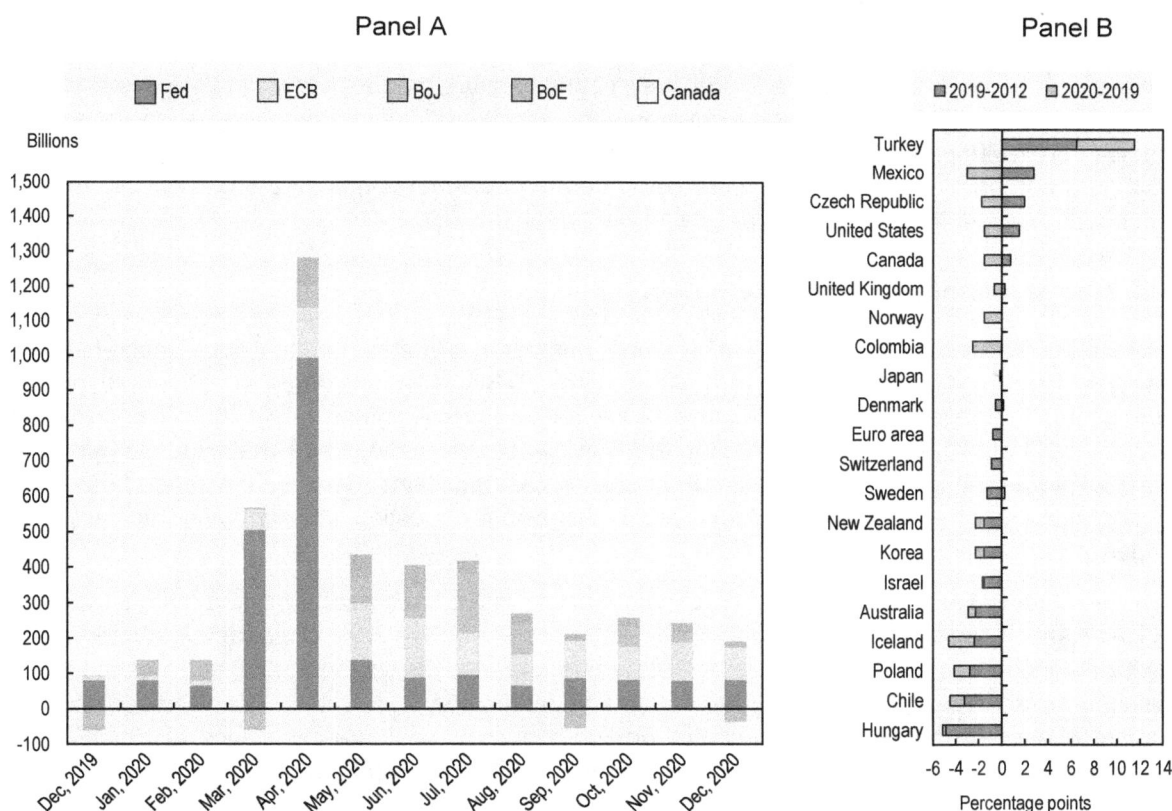

Note: Converted into USD at the end of each month. Calculated from data on security holdings for the Federal Reserve and the BoJ. For the BoE data are calculated from holdings of gilts by the Bank of England's asset purchase facility. Data for ECB are net purchases for the PSPP and the PEPP.
Source: Central banks and OECD calculations.

1.3.2. Growing number of new maturity lines and new instruments

In 2020, many governments have increased the issuance of securities across the yield curve, and introduced new maturity lines. Increased budget deficits created room for issuance of additional securities, as the large funding needs allowed the volume of new bonds to be built-up in a relatively short period without reducing the volume of existing ones. The OECD survey on primary market developments revealed that 20 out of 34 respondent OECD countries issued either new types of securities or new maturity lines in 2020. Furthermore, 15 countries are planning to do so in 2021. While a number of countries, including Belgium, the Czech Republic, Israel, Sweden and the United States issued new longer-dated securities in 2020, some small issuers including Denmark and New Zealand issued euro-denominated debt.

Another important examples for new instruments are retail bonds and green bonds. For example, Italy offered a new 10-year maturity bond called 'BTP Futura' to retail investors, the proceeds of which to be used to fund coronavirus measures. Germany, Hungary and Sweden launched green bonds in 2020; and Canada, Iceland, Italy, Spain and the United Kingdom are planning to issue in 2021. It should be noted that the countries that launched sovereign green bonds in 2020 made the decision on the introduction of green bonds as a new funding instrument before the COVID-19 crisis. The upsurge in government funding needs due to the pandemic have helped the issuers to increase the volume of the inaugural issuance of the green bonds in 2020.

From a debt management perspective, issuing a new instrument helps to enhance the financing capacity of sovereigns and to diversify their funding sources. Depending on their maturity structure, incorporation of long-dated securities is also useful to moderate interest rate and rollover risks, and is especially useful when the yield curve is fairly flat. In addition, green bonds feature broader benefits to the overall economy and the financial market by supporting governments' efforts in financing the low-carbon transition and promoting the development of a domestic market for green bonds. Despite its rapid growth, the size of the sovereign green bond market is quite small compared to traditional bonds. In the OECD area, sovereign green bonds account for only 0.2% of all government debt securities.

1.3.3. Heavy reliance on short-term debt issuance

T-Bill markets, typically used for cash management purposes, are often the most liquid markets and offer cheap financing conditions. Because of these features, T-Bills are considered as 'shock absorbers' by sovereign debt managers (Box 1.1) and played a key role in sovereign financing in 2020. The uncertainties associated with public expenditure related to the COVID-19 crisis have posed challenges for government cash-flow forecasting and management of the resulting cash positions resulted in increased use of short-term debt instruments. Many sovereigns issued T-Bills also for boosting liquidity buffers against possible changes in cash needs.

Given the funding flexibility T-Bills, offer, the bulk of the initial cash needs of governments due to the COVID-19 shock were financed through T-bill issuance. More than 70% of pandemic-related debt has been issued in the form of T-Bills in France, Germany, Japan and the United States, at almost no cost (e.g. negative 6-month Treasury bill yields in euro area and Japan, and 0.1% in the United States). As a result, the share of short-term instruments in central government marketable debt issuance in the OECD area, which averaged 40% in the past five years, increased to 48% in 2020 (Figure 1.8).

While the initial borrowing needs were predominantly met through T-bill issuance, sovereign issuers have been increasing long-term bond issuances steadily as a prudent means of managing their maturity profile and limiting potential future issuance volatility. This also aims at rebuilding contingency capacity in the event that significant funding is needed again in short order. The 2020 survey on Central Government Marketable Debt and Borrowing projects the share of long-term debt to increase by more than 2 percentage points in 2021 to reach 54.4% at the end of the year. However, it should be noted that governments' ability to rebalance their issuance towards long-dated bonds may be constrained in the short-term by the large size of the financing needs and limits to investor demand for duration.

Figure 1.8. Maturity composition of central government marketable debt issuance

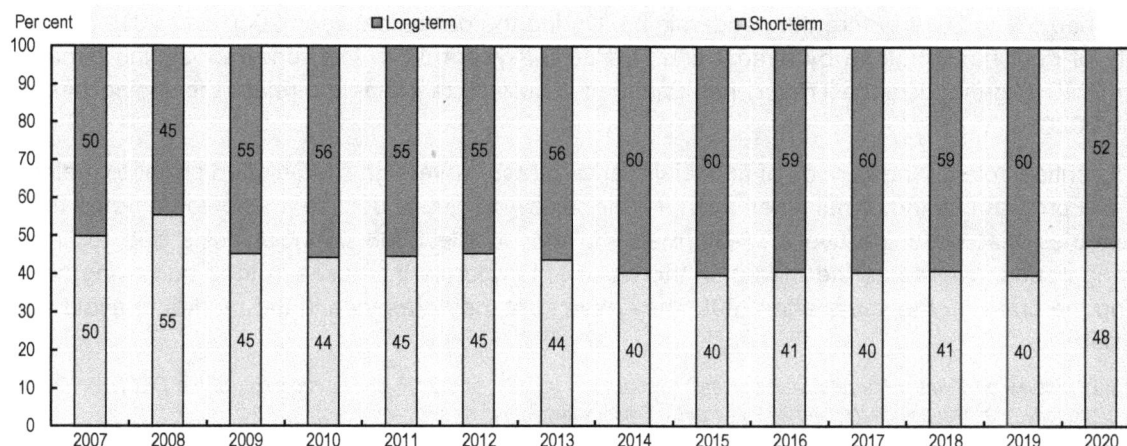

Notes: This is based on standardised gross borrowing.
Source: 2020 Survey on Central Government Marketable Debt and Borrowing; OECD Economic Outlook (December 2020); Refinitiv; national authorities' websites; and OECD calculations.

Box 1.1. Issuance of T-Bills to navigate shocks

T-Bills are typically considered as 'shock absorbers' by sovereign issuers. In case of an unexpected rise in funding requirements during a crisis, they tend to borrow more from the T-Bill markets. There are demand and supply factors for this: From the demand side, investors generally desire the safest, most liquid assets in times of crises, in particular for T-Bills. This leads to a larger decline in the yields on T-Bills, and results in cheaper financing conditions. From the supply side, under such circumstances there are often uncertainties regarding the size and duration of revenue shortfalls and expenses related to governments support measures. Issuing short-term instruments helps managing uncertainties regarding the financing requirement, some of which may be temporary. Considered together, both factors make this strategy consistent with the DMO's goal of funding government at the lowest cost over time.

Despite its advantages, a heavy and continued reliance on short-term financing amplifies near-term refinancing risk, as maturing debt needs to be refinanced several times within a short period of time at new market interest rates. When conditions improve, DMOs should consider gradually shifting from money markets to capital markets (i.e. to longer-term bonds) in order to regain their emergency response capacity and reduce rollover risk in the medium and long term.

During the 2008 financial crisis, OECD area DMOs increased T-Bill issuance to finance the unexpected increase in borrowing needs. More than 55 % of gross borrowing needs for 2008 is covered by issuing short-term debt. In the following years, there had been a gradual shift towards longer dated maturities to mitigate the rollover risk. The share of short-term debt issuance in total gross issuance fell gradually between 2010 and 2019, and was 40% on average in 2019 with large cross country differences. For example, in the United States, where T-Bills have historically played an important role in financing, their share rose to 84% of total marketable debt issuance in 2008, before declining significantly in the subsequent years. The US Treasury followed a similar strategy during the COVID-19 crisis, when the share of T-Bill issuance in marketable securities increased from about 75% in 2019 to 80% in 2020.

France has also had similar experience both in the 2008 financial crisis period and in 2020. The share of T-Bills (BTFs, Bons du Trésor à taux fixe et à intérêts précomptés) in total debt jumped from 8.5% in 2007 to 13.6% in 2008 and 18.7% in 2009. This ratio had been reduced gradually in the following years, and reached 6% in 2019 before the pandemic hit. During the period between 2010 and 2019 average maturity of debt has lengthen by almost one year to 8.2 years. With this renewed issuing capacity, French DMO (Agence France Trésor) has financed a bulk of its pandemic related financing through BTFs in 2020.

Given its critical role during periods of financial market stress, sovereign DMOs often prefer to maintain their T-Bill programme in normal times even if their borrowing needs decline. It should be noted that a few countries that were inactive in T-Bill markets prior to the 2008 financial crisis due to limited borrowing needs, re-entered the market in the wake of temporary increases in their borrowing needs following the crisis. In the years after 2008, they have kept their presence in the market to avoid a re-entry cost.

Source: *2020 Survey on Primary Markets Developments, discussions in 2009 and 2020 annual meetings of the OECD WPDM, US Treasury's quarterly refunding documents and Agence France Trésor's key figures on short-term debt.*

1.3.4. Borrowing operations have been adapted to rapidly changing circumstances

OECD sovereign issuers take the decision on issuance strategies, methods and procedures on the back of a comprehensive assessment of market demand, size of the annual financing needs, ability to access to different markets, and market segments. Due to the impact of the pandemic on market conditions and yield curves, sovereign issues have adjusted borrowing strategies and communications formats to rapidly changing circumstances, in some cases methods and procedures as well. While most of the OECD area debt offices consider recent adjustments to the borrowing strategies temporarily, some of them have made permanent changes in particular regarding auction calendars, frequency of auctions and the use of syndications (Table 1.1).

Table 1.1. Temporary and long-term strategy changes in the wake of the pandemic

	Temporary strategy changes	More permanent longer term strategy
Auctions		
Auction calendar	18 yes; 13 no	6 yes; 22 no
Frequency of auctions	20 higher; 0 lower; 13 no change	7 higher; 0 lower; 22 no change
Post-auction option facility (non-competitive bids)	4 higher; 1 lower; 18 no change	4 higher; 1 lower; 17 no change
Other issuance techniques		
Use of syndications	16 higher; 0 lower; 16 no change	6 higher; 1 lower; 23 no change
Use of private placements	8 higher; 1 lower; 12 no change	1 higher; 1 lower; 16 no change

Note: Based on the responses from 35 OECD countries.
Source: 2020 Survey on primary market developments.

A major challenge for many DMOs has been cash flow forecasting and management of the sharp and unexpected changes in government funding needs throughout the year. Another issue has been the quality of price discovery at auctions due to heightened uncertainty. In response, several issuers have taken actions to adapt their borrowing operations to facilitate the primary market distribution process. While auctions remained the key means of selling government securities in the markets throughout the crisis, size and number of auctions have increased considerably across the OECD area. In many countries, other issuance techniques such as syndications and private placements have also been expanded since the pandemic (Table 1.1). Other changes include increasing supplementary non-competitive post-auction option facility in auctions (e.g. Italy, Turkey and the United Kingdom), which aims to ease price discovery challenge faced by primary dealers during stressed market conditions.

A recent survey of primary market developments amongst OECD sovereign issuers revealed that one-third of the sovereign issuers increased the issuance of securities across the yield curve. In addition, around half of the countries, including Australia, Germany and Italy, have been making more use of syndications in the wake of the COVID-19 crisis. Syndications enabled DMOs to sell large amounts of securities in a short period of time without creating additional pressure on primary dealers (see Box 1.2 for a detailed discussion on the use of syndications). For example, in 2020, this procedure was used to cover around 10% of sovereign funding needs in the United Kingdom and 20% in Australia, Belgium and Portugal. Similar to syndications, private placements are often used as a complementary selling technique to auctions. In 2020, a number of small issuers such as Finland and Slovenia increased the use of private placements to raise large volumes of funds. One advantage of private placements is that there is a direct sale between the issuer and the buyer, so there is no agency fee. However, disadvantages such as the loss of transparency and heavy documentation requirements during issuance prevent the widespread use of the method.

Box 1.2. Use of syndications in sovereign debt management

The syndication procedure is an issuing method whereby a DMO initially appoints a single or a group of financial institutions (the "Lead Manager(s)") for subscription of the bonds to be issued and sold on to final investors. Since the late 1990s, this issuance method has been used in both advanced and less advanced sovereign markets. Today, syndications are part of the toolbox in a majority of sovereign debt management offices (DMOs) in the OECD area.

The role of syndications in sovereign funding programmes varies greatly. For most sovereign issuers such as France, Italy and the United Kingdom, they serve as a complementary tool to auctions. As such, even when the use of syndications increases at times of financial stress, sovereign funding through syndications is often limited compared to total funding needs (i.e. less than 15-20% of total annual borrowings). On the other hand, for a few smaller issuers such as Belgium, Ireland and Slovenia, syndications play a more important role in sovereign funding programmes. Major motivations for using syndications are the following:

- *Issuance of a new security or a new tenor:* In order to facilitate the price discovery process and to some extent get more marketing service, syndications are preferred when launching a new security or a new tenor, particularly at the long end of the yield curve. For example, Canada issued a new 50-year bond, and France issued a debut green bond in 2017 via syndications. In Finland, almost half of the long-term issuance, all of which are new lines, is executed in syndicated format in 2020. Also, they are used for issuing foreign currency denominated bonds in international markets (e.g. Canada, Denmark, Poland and Turkey).

- *To support primary dealership systems:* DMOs use syndications to motivate primary dealers in their role of supporting primary and secondary markets of government securities. They often rank primary dealers based on their performance in primary and secondary market of government securities and top scoring banks get more syndication business and usually longer deals (e.g. France and Germany).

- *To provide flexibility in the financing of newly introduced programmes:* Syndications are useful to sell relatively large amount of securities in a short period of time. In the event of unexpected funding needs, or in times of turbulence, it becomes critical to have a tool in place to meet governments' financing needs in a reliable fashion without putting extra pressure on the primary dealers. Use of syndications are intended to serve this purpose. It also supports predictability of auction programmes by enabling DMOs to raise funds without changing their regular auction calendars.

In terms of operational aspects, a single or a group of financial institutions (e.g. often between three and six) called 'Joint Lead Managers' is designated to fulfil the role of book runner, to provide certainty of funds and intermediate the transaction between the issuer and investors. Some DMOs appoint co-leads with the principal objective of enlarging the order book. When selecting lead managers (and co-leads), DMOs consider a number of factors, including their annual performance in primary and secondary markets of government securities, distribution capabilities and their expertise in a specific market segment (e.g. green bonds). In some cases, rotation among the candidate banks is considered as well in the selection process.

Regarding the disadvantages, DMOs highlight two issues: costs stemming from fees and administrative preparations. Unlike auctions, syndications involve intermediation costs as lead managers demand fees for their service. These fees are usually small and linked to the size of the transaction and duration of the bond (e.g. France, Finland, Italy and the UK). In addition, some difficulties arise in terms of the administrative preparation and of the execution of the operations, as the process requires more human resources than auctions.

Source: *OECD WPDM survey on design and implementation of syndications (2013), AOFM Investor insights (2019) and discussions held at the 2017 and 2020 annual meetings of the WPDM.*

The COVID-19 pandemic has also put pressure on the operational capacity of DMOs in most countries, in particular where widespread remote work is taking place under lockdown measures. Although pandemics per se were not amongst the business interruption scenarios in many OECD country DMOs (except Colombia, Ireland, Japan and Switzerland) before the pandemic, all include arrangements to ensure business continuity in the event that their office is not available for use. Hence, they successfully activated their business continuity plans (BCPs) in the early stages of the outbreak (OECD, 2020[2]). Thereby, they managed to ensure the continuity of the funding and cash management activities, which are critical for the continuity of governments' fight against the pandemic.

The pandemic forced sovereign issuers to change their communication format and strategy. DMOs have updated investors more frequently through digital communication tools (e.g. email distribution lists, publishing market notices on their websites, virtual meetings and phone calls) regarding changes in funding needs and plans in response to the COVID-19 crisis. In addition, senior government officials (e.g. Ministers, treasury secretaries and heads of DMOs) have communicated actively on how they evaluate the developments and address the risks to ensure proper functioning of government securities markets.

Many DMOs made adjustments in quarterly and annual auction calendars, reflecting modifications of various aspects of their financing plans. Given the level of uncertainty associated with expenditure on COVID-19 and its impact on the economy, especially at the initial stage of the crisis, it was not feasible for many countries to estimate their financing requirements for the whole financial year of 2020. In this regard, some DMOs have taken a cautious approach in communicating the uncertainty around new funding needs as well as revisions to refinancing strategies. The UK government, for example, reflected the high degree of uncertainty about both the size and pace of financing required to meet the costs of COVID-19, by announcing , a series of partial in-year extensions to its financing requirements on an exceptional basis. Accordingly, the United Kingdom has implemented a series of matching extensions to its programme of gilt operations. Notwithstanding the necessity of the adjustments during a crisis, sovereign debt managers stressed that the temporary nature of some adjustments should be communicated clearly with investors to avoid potential misinterpretations, as well as reputational damage.

1.4. Sovereign debt ratios reached all-time highs in many countries

The fiscal policy response of governments to the COVID-19 crisis has substantially increased sovereign debt levels across the OECD area. In absolute terms, outstanding central government debt for the OECD area is expected to increase from USD 47 trillion in 2019 to USD 55.7 trillion in 2020 as a result of the surge in new financing needs. While fiscal support measures are expected to continue in most countries, albeit at a lower scale, debt is projected to further increase to USD 61 trillion by the end of 2021 (Figure 1.9).

Figure 1.9. Outstanding central government marketable debt in OECD countries, 2007-2021, nominal and as a percentage of GDP

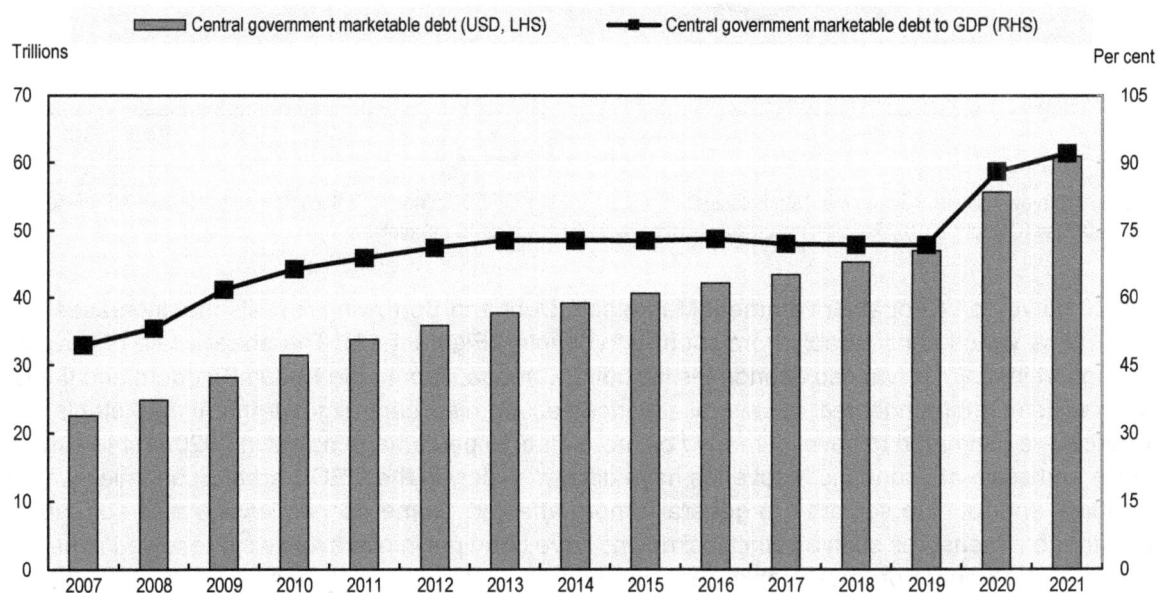

Source: 2020 Survey on Central Government Marketable Debt and Borrowing; OECD Economic Outlook (December 2020); IMF World Economic Outlook Database (October 2020); Refinitiv, national authorities' websites and OECD calculations.

Having increased sharply from 2008 to 2013, the outstanding debt-to-GDP ratio for the OECD area had somewhat stabilised before the pandemic hit in 2020. Despite increasing gross borrowing needs for the whole OECD area, the effect on the debt-to-GDP ratio was limited, largely due to favourable interest rate-growth differentials in most OECD countries (OECD, 2019[3]). As discussed in Section 1.1, economies have been hard-hit by the COVID-19 pandemic despite unprecedented efforts by governments across the OECD. While fiscal balances deteriorated by around 10% of GDP, the OECD-area economy contracted by 5.5%. A combination of rising fiscal deficits and contracting economies pushed government debt-to-GDP ratios up significantly. Central government marketable debt-to-GDP ratios for the OECD area are estimated to have increased by 16 percentage points to over 88% in 2020 (Figure 1.9). This is nearly twice the impact of the 2008 financial crisis (Figure 1.10). Going forward, OECD economies are expected to gain momentum while fiscal supports are set to continue at a lower scale, the government debt-to-GDP ratio is projected to increase by at least 4 percentage points in 2021. Projections for 2021 depend on various factors, including the roll out of vaccination campaigns and the stringency of containment measures. A large-scale vaccination deployment would allow an easing of containment measures and would strengthen confidence. Under this scenario, fiscal plans may remain unchanged. However, if large-scale containment measures remain in place and potential additional fiscal policy support needs to be pursued, then, the debt-to-GDP ratio may increase further in 2021.

Figure 1.10. Marketable debt-to-GDP: 2008 financial crisis vs COVID-19 shock

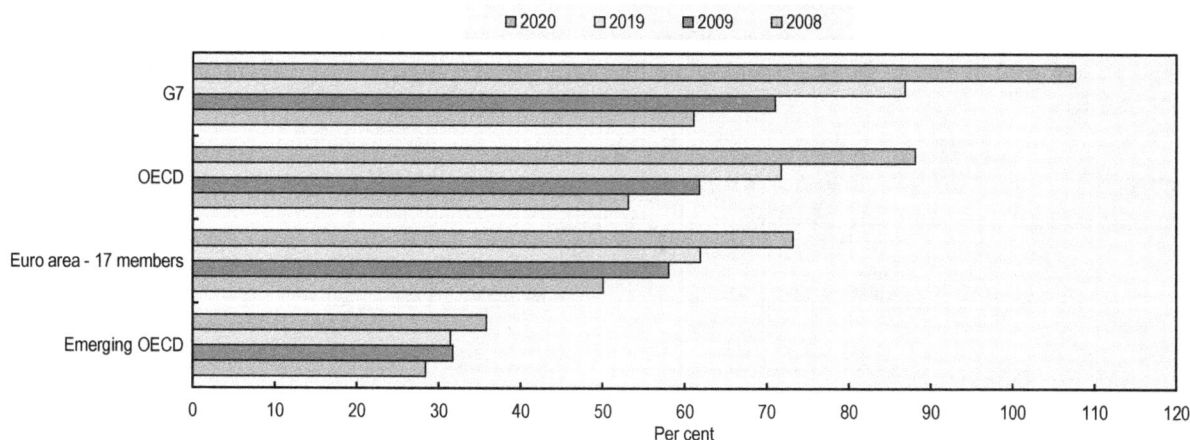

Source: 2020 Survey on Central Government Marketable Debt and Borrowing; OECD Economic Outlook (December 2020); IMF World Economic Outlook Database (October 2020); Refinitiv, national authorities' websites and OECD calculations.

The 2020 survey on Central Government Marketable Debt and Borrowing reveals that increases in debt-to-GDP ratios varied considerably from country to country (Figure 1.11). The sheer scale of government fiscal support in major advanced economies including Canada, Japan, the United Kingdom and the United States has been unprecedented. In several advanced economies, central government marketable debt-to-GDP ratios are estimated to have increased by more than 15 percentage points in 2020. At the same time, the pace and scale of economic recoveries have differed widely in the OECD area. Economies with larger hospitability and tourism sectors are generally more affected. Some economies are also suffering more where stringent measures such as strict lockdowns have been put in place following renewed virus surges. Conversely, the impact on marketable debt has been limited in some cases, in particular where fiscal support has been provided in the form of loan guarantees, and complemented by the use of available government funds rather than security issuances. For example, central government marketable debt-to-GDP ratios are estimated to have risen less than 7 percentage points in some countries, including Ireland, Korea, Latvia and Sweden.

The pandemic has highlighted the challenge for policy makers to strike the right balance: while they strive to support the economy with fiscal policy measures and limit the damage caused by the pandemic, the potential implications of rising sovereign debt levels need to be taken into consideration for long-term debt sustainability. Debt sustainability depends fundamentally on the interest rate any country pays on its debt; its capacity to generate primary balances and long-term growth trajectories. Currently, nominal interest rates are lower than nominal economic growth, allowing economic recoveries to be supported by deficit generating fiscal measures. At the same time, long-term economic growth depends on the efficient use of government expenditure on growth-enhancing investments so that they do not turn into recurring budget items. To this end, the *OECD Economic Outlook of December 2020* concluded that although this new environment requires the use of fiscal policy, fiscal stimulus should be well-targeted going forward to enhance resilience and support future economic growth.

Figure 1.11. Changes in central government marketable debt-to-GDP ratios in selected OECD countries

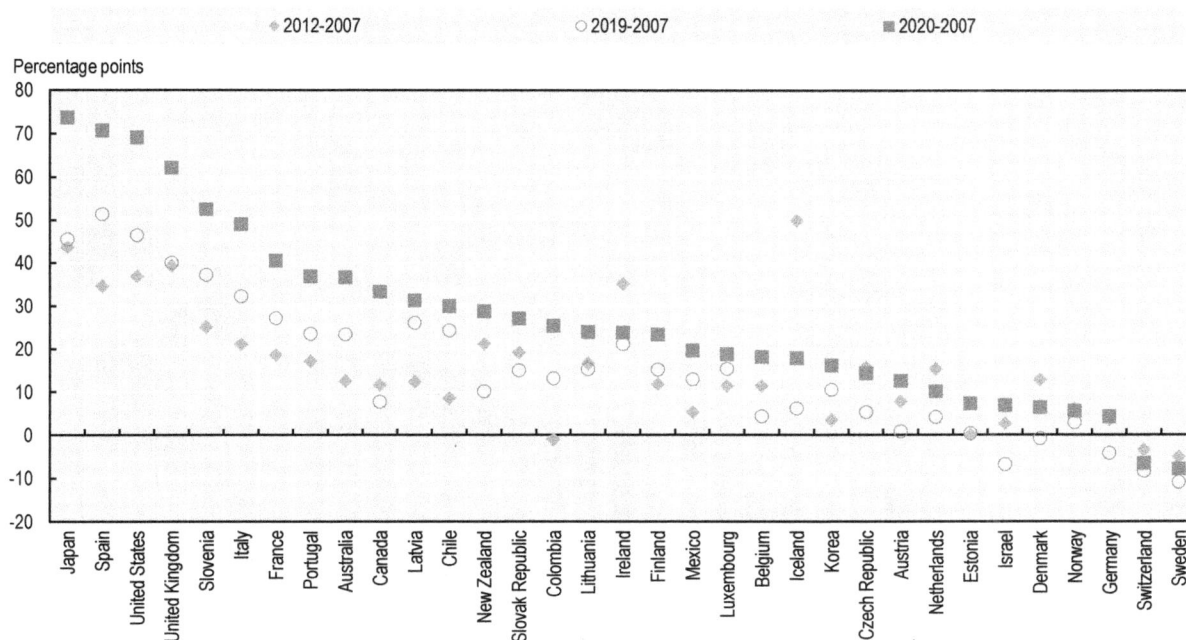

Source: 2020 Survey on Central Government Marketable Debt and Borrowing; OECD Economic Outlook (December 2020); IMF World Economic Outlook Database (October 2020); Refinitiv, national authorities' websites and OECD calculations.

1.4.1. Prolonged low interest rates have contained the impact of higher financing needs on government interest expenses

Thanks to prolonged low interest rates, OECD governments have paid less on their debt in recent years, even though sovereign debt levels are high and on an upward trend in many countries. Despite this surge in borrowing amounts provoked by the COVID-19 crisis, interest expense on outstanding government debt continued to fall in most countries in 2020. Figure 1.12 illustrates the percentage of government interest expenditure in GDP in 2007 and in 2020. Interest expenditure in relation to GDP in this period fell by around 50% in ten countries (including Austria, Belgium, France and Germany); and more than 25% in seven countries, remaining stable and slightly increased in some countries. For example, in the United States, government interest expense-to-GDP remained broadly stable (4.2% in 2020), despite the significant increase in government debt during this period.

Going forward, sovereign financing needs will be subject to sizeable changes as a result of governments' ongoing response to the COVID-19 crisis and its effects on economic activity and government revenues. Interest rates are likely to remain low in the short-to-medium term and continue to help reducing the cost of financing public debt. While being an advantage for sovereign issuers, the associated prospects of low financial returns can harm long-term investors. For example, low returns on fixed-income assets may weigh on the value of pension reserve funds (OECD, 2020[4]).

Figure 1.12. General government interest expenses in relation to GDP in selected OECD countries

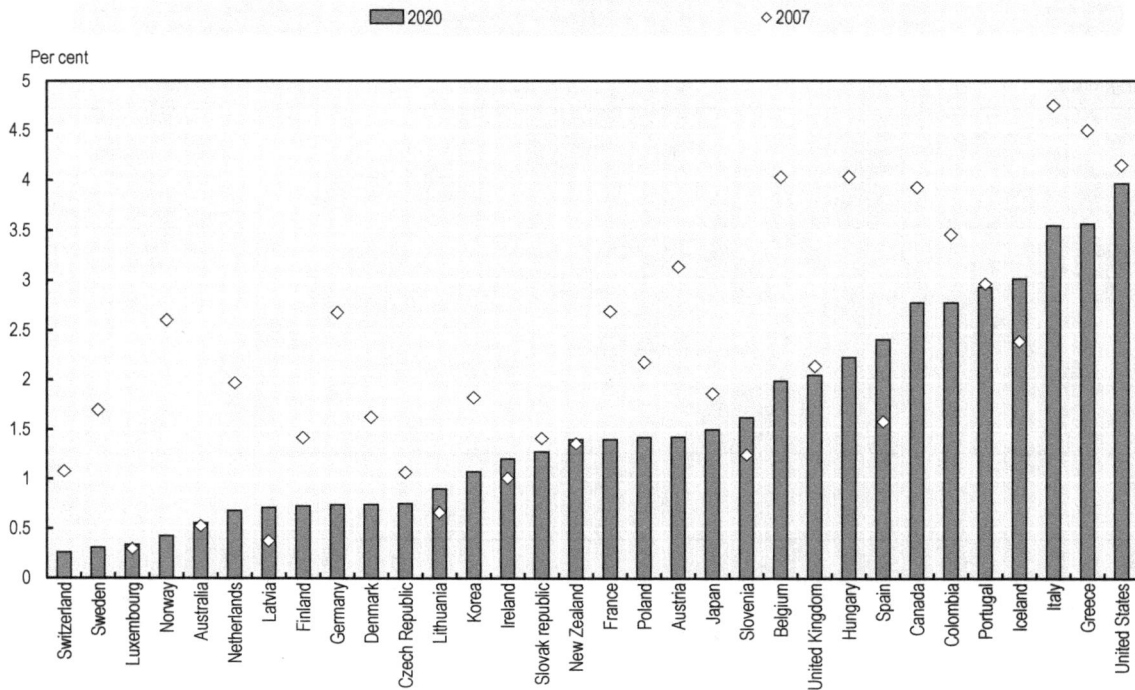

Notes: Gross general government interest payments to GDP
Source: OECD Economic Outlook (December 2020); and OECD calculations.

1.4.2. The average maturity of outstanding debt has dropped from the pre-pandemic peaks in most countries

Sovereign issuers in many OECD countries have expanded their short-term borrowing programmes to manage unexpected surges in financing needs in the wake of the COVID-19 pandemic. Shortened borrowing maturity during 2020 was apparent in the maturity composition of outstanding debt. The share of short-term instruments in outstanding central government marketable debt in the OECD area, which averaged 10% in the past five years, increased to 15% in 2020 (Figure 1.13).

Before the COVID-19 crisis, high indebtedness was accompanied by higher average term-to-maturity (ATM) in most OECD countries. The average ATMs, which have been extended in recent years, shrank in 2020. After extending by 1.7 years between 2007 and 2019, the ATM declined slightly from 7.9 years to 7.7 years, with striking differences across countries (Figure 1.14). In most countries including Canada, Denmark, Japan, the United Kingdom and the United States, the ATM of outstanding debt decreased in 2020 as a result of increased share of short-term debt in annual borrowing programmes. In the United States, for example, the average term-maturity of debt declined from 70 months in 2019 to 65 months in 2020. In some countries, such as Israel, Greece, Hungary and Mexico, the ATMs have lengthened considerably due to the issuance of long-term foreign-currency-denominated bonds. After a long break, Estonia and Luxembourg issued bonds in the financial markets in 2020 for budget financing purposes. The average maturity of the debt stock of some countries, including Australia, Italy, Ireland and France, remained the same as in 2019.

Figure 1.13. Maturity structure of central government marketable debt

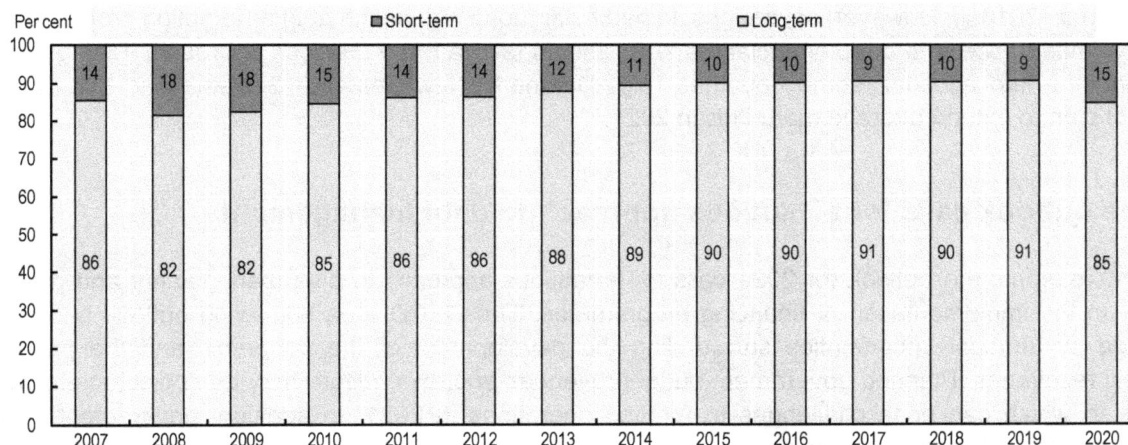

Source: 2020 Survey on Central Government Marketable Debt and Borrowing; OECD Economic Outlook (December 2020); IMF World Economic Outlook Database (October 2020); Refinitiv, national authorities' websites and OECD calculations.

Figure 1.14. Average term-to-maturity of outstanding marketable debt in OECD countries

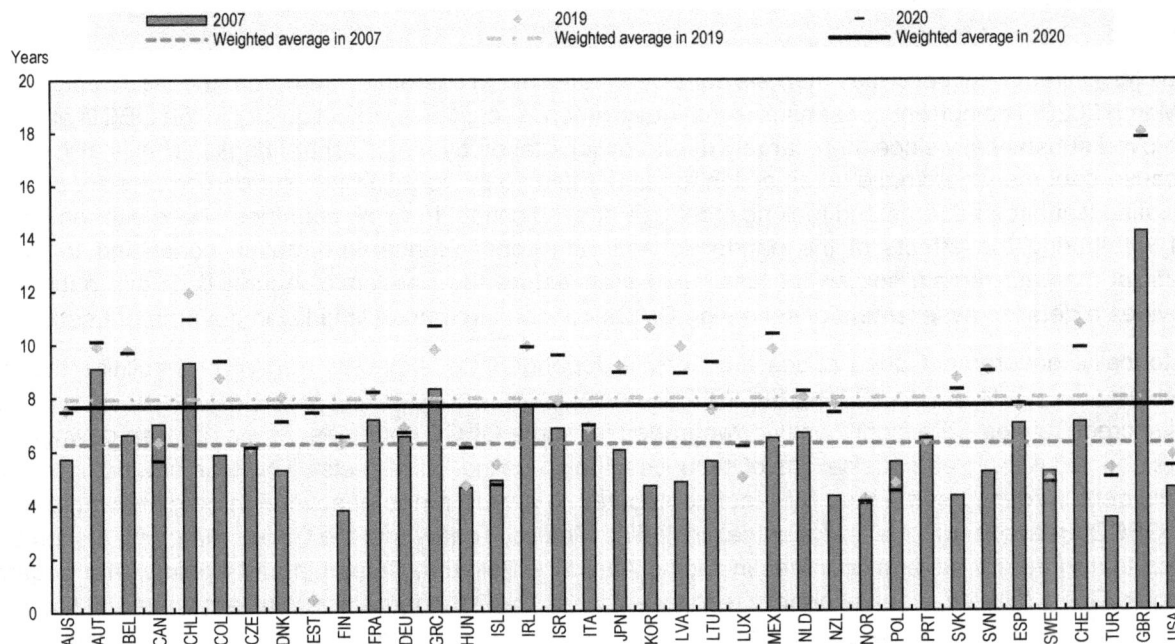

Note: See Annex 1.A for country specific notes.
Source: 2020 Survey on Central Government Marketable Debt and Borrowing.

As discussed in previous editions of this publication, average maturities have important implications in terms of how much of the debt has to be refinanced in the short and medium term. From a risk management perspective, higher ATM and duration figures imply a lower pass-through impact of interest rate changes on government interest costs and enhanced fiscal resilience. This is less of a concern for sovereigns with economic flexibility and access to deep and liquid financial markets. Those countries might benefit from shortening borrowing maturities in order to take advantage of very low short-term rates (Maravalle and Rawdanowicz, 2018[5]). However, sovereigns, in particular those with a high debt redemption profile and/or relatively limited access to deep financial markets, should take a more cautious approach. Taking these considerations into account, some countries (e.g. Denmark, New Zealand, Slovenia and the Slovak Republic) plan to extend average maturities in 2021.

1.5. The outlook calls for a cautious approach to debt management

For many reasons, the outlook for 2021 calls for a cautious approach to debt management and greater flexibility in the implementation of financing programmes. The OECD area borrowing outlook has been hampered by unusual uncertainties surrounding the development of the pandemic and the pace of economic recoveries. Planned government budget revenues and expenditure may be subject to sizeable changes to which can pose challenges to funding operations in 2021. In addition, governments may introduce new fiscal packages to support economic recoveries. Depending on the extent of the changes, the planned size and timing of government funding needs are subject to modification.

The increased gross funding requirements brought high rollover ratios, and high average auction sizes in many OECD countries. This elevates potential vulnerability to market disruptions and other event risks. Amid persistent uncertainty, sovereign debt management offices are advised to diligently set out their annual financing programmes with careful consideration of expected events (monetary policy announcements, elections etc.), scheduled payments and the maturity profile of the debt stock. They should also ensure their emergency response capacities are adequate. This is important not only for smooth execution of financing plans, but also for the smooth functioning of financial markets at critical times.

Thus far, government securities markets have been functioning smoothly, apart from the market disruption in March 2020. The current consensus is that government securities market liquidity in the OECD area has improved substantially since then, largely due to actions taken by major central banks. This is also in part because debt managers have taken action to make them so by, for example, supporting primary dealers, adjusting issuance patterns and making more use of syndication. In some countries where economies are still weathering the effects of the pandemic and with consequential information continuing to arrive, financial markets remain somewhat less liquid than before the pandemic. Annex B of this publication provides a detailed assessment of sovereign DMOs concerning market liquidity in government securities.

Historically, government bond prices are heavily dependent on expected default probabilities that are measured by credit ratings. During the 2008 financial crisis, and following the euro area sovereign debt crisis, credit ratings were significantly downgraded for some OECD countries. Some of these downgrades were coupled with deleterious selloffs of securities, the so-called "cliff effects". This time around, increased public debt burdens have – thus far – not contributed to a wide range of sovereign credit downgrades in the OECD area, except for a few countries including Mexico, Turkey and the United Kingdom. It should be noted that there are several countries including Australia, Belgium, Colombia and Spain with a negative outlook. Going forward, weak economic recoveries, weak credit fundamentals with large external financing requirements and low reserve buffers can put strong downward pressure on sovereign credit ratings, which in turn may amplify vulnerabilities resulting from high sovereign and corporate debt levels. From debt management perspective, strengthened sovereign debt compositions in terms of maturity, interest rate and currency composition can help mitigate vulnerability concerns.

1.5.1. Rollover ratios as well as auction sizes are rising in many countries

An important aspect of governments' annual financing programme is related to the percentage of debt to be refinanced (i.e. rollover), and distribution of this refinancing needs over various instruments through different issuance mechanisms. In the OECD area, augmented re-financing needs in addition to new financing needs resulted in sizeable increases in gross financing needs. In addition, the sharp increase in short-term debt issuance in 2020 has resulted in higher rollover ratios near-term. Although the low interest rate environment has facilitated the financing of budget deficits as well as the re-financing of existing debt in recent years, deteriorated roll over ratios may pose challenges for some countries depending on the additional financing needs that may occur during the year. In the United States, for example, the percentage of debt maturing in the next 12 months jumped from 27% in 2019 to 35% in 2020, as a result of increased T-Bill financing in 2020.

Figure 1.15 illustrates that one quarter of total stock of government securities is due in the next 12 months. In the next three years, governments will need to refinance around 45% of their outstanding marketable debt. This ratio was around 40% in the five years to end-2019. While rollover ratios indicate financing needs relative to repayments, they should be considered together with absolute volumes of scheduled redemptions. Due to fast accumulation of debt, redemption volumes have also increased significantly. Lower average maturities, accompanied by higher volume of redemptions often brings about challenging repayment schedules, and weakens investors' confidence. In the view of high rollover ratios, the size of governments' auctions in many countries are expected to remain substantial in 2021.

Figure 1.15. Redemptions of central government marketable debt in OECD country groupings, as a percentage of debt stock

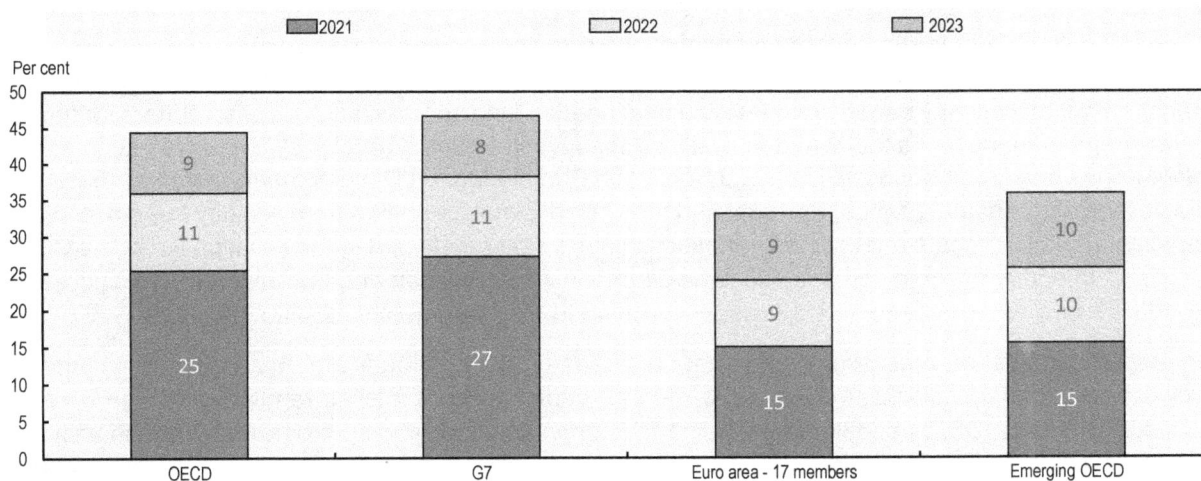

Note: Using the debt comparable application data, calculated on current USD amounts outstanding.
Source: Refinitiv.

While a one-off shock to the level of debt may not on its own endanger long-term debt sustainability given the current low interest rate environment, a sustained period of high volatility could cause rollover risks for sovereigns, and debt may have to be rolled over at high cost. From a debt management perspective, the refinancing risk (i.e. a risk that debt might have to be refinanced at very high rates, or in the extreme case, cannot be rolled over at all) can be addressed by rebalancing the debt profile of the issuance programmes by incorporating more long-term instruments depending on market conditions. Several DMOs in the OECD area have already made important progress in this direction. For example, the Czech Republic started executing switch auctions in October 2020, whereby it buys back T-Bills and issues long-term government bonds. The main aim of this operation is to adjust the redemption profile of debt in favour of long-term government bonds. Further discussion of managing refinancing risk is provided in Chapter 2.

In view of fast debt accumulation, rebalancing of debt portfolio maturities should be considered to ease near-term redemption pressures and strengthen the resilience of the debt portfolio against refinancing risk. A lengthening of government debt maturities may also facilitate a smooth exit of expansionary monetary policies, when policy rates eventually rise in the future (Bartsch et al., n.d.[6]). With lengthened maturities, this rise will be slowly passed on to the debt service and help to avoid endogenous debt accumulation.[9]

Increased refinancing needs also have implications for the banks that serve as primary dealers. As repeatedly discussed in the previous editions of this publication, regulatory reforms triggered by the 2008 financial crisis have improved financial stability, but at the same time have limited the appetite of bank dealers to warehouse investor flows on their balance sheets. While central banks have helped to absorb additional supply of government securities in the market in major advanced economies, the balance sheet capacity of primary dealers may need to be assessed more carefully in planning governments funding.

Country experiences suggest that complementing auctions with other issuance techniques such as syndications and private placements are useful for easing the pressure on primary dealership systems and providing flexibility in the execution of issuance programmes. In addition, having access to different funding sources such as foreign financing would supplement the issuance in local markets and reduce financial crowding out risks (Priftis and Zimic, 2021[7]). For euro area countries, funds from the European Union in particular loans from the SURE fund and the Next Generation EU Recovery Fund which aim to deal with the epidemic, will also contribute to alleviating the pressure on local markets, in particular primary dealers.[10]

1.5.2. Emergency response capacities

While the outlook remains uncertain and confidence remains fragile despite positive news on the vaccine front, having emergency funding tools in place is relevant for all sovereign issuers. Sovereign debt management offices may benefit from building contingency funding tools, such as cash buffers for flexibility increasing the financing capacity and diversifying the investor base through new securities such as long-dated bonds and green bonds.[11] The 2020 Survey on Primary Market Developments indicates that several DMOs including Austria, France, Portugal and the United States benefited from liquidity buffers in 2020, in particular used to mitigate unexpected variations in borrowing needs during the initial phase of the COVID-19 crisis. In addition, some countries such as Germany, Italy, Sweden and the United States successfully introduced new types of securities without diminishing trading volumes of existing securities.

An important part of emergency response activities is to communicate the changes in financing programmes to stakeholders, including the general public. In their role as regular and large issuers in securities markets, DMOs should carefully manage changes in borrowing programmes by balancing the need for transparency and predictability while allowing for sufficient room for manoeuvre. Risks to financing programmes especially when they occur prior to an auction, poses a challenge for transparency and predictability and could cause reputational damage if not well managed. To this end, sovereign debt managers should remain vigilant in monitoring market developments and market participants carefully and closely in case of an event risk. Additional communication with market participants may be required to convey changes in borrowing plans.

Crises conditions require strong coordination and communication with fiscal and monetary policy authorities. In particular, a timely update of cash flow forecasts are critical for sovereign issuers to identify the volume and immediacy of funding needs. This requires efficient communication channels between cash managers and their counterparts in spending and revenue collection agencies. At a time when market liquidity becomes more sensitive in financial markets, communication with monetary authorities regarding government cash balances and borrowing strategies, in particular with respects to debt redemption projections, and any change in cash buffer targets, could be critical in avoiding unnecessary pressure on market liquidity.

Furthermore, sovereign DMOs should regularly conduct business impact analysis to keep pace with the evolving risks such as cyberattacks and have an effective business continuity plan in light of the lessons learned during the COVID-19 crisis. Identification of gaps in business continuity and disaster recovery plans would help to improve preparedness in case of an emergency or an event risk. An important component of the revisions should be about key person risk. Cross-team training of more staff with critical skills through virtual classes and webinars to avoid key person risk (e.g. staff involved in cash market operations, derivative markets and debt repayments) can enhance emergency response capacity of debt management offices. In addition, the use and priority of secondary sites may be worth reviewing as the recent experience of wide-scale remote working has proved effective in managing certain type of stress scenarios.

References

AOFM (2019), "Bond issuance methods - Tenders vs Syndications", *AOFM Investor Insights*, https://www.aofm.gov.au/investors/wholesale-investors/investor-insights/bond-issuance-methods-tenders-versus-syndications. [14]

Bartsch, E. et al. (n.d.), "It's all in the mix: how can monetary and fiscal policies work or fail together?", *Geneva Report on the World Economy* No 23. [6]

Cohen, D. and S. Villemot (2011), "Endogenous debt crises", Vol. CEPR Discussion Paper 8270. [19]

Corsetti, G. and L. Dedola (2013), "The Mystery of the Printing Press: Self-fulfilling debt crises and monetary sovereignty", *CEPR Discussion Paper*, Vol. 9358, https://cepr.org/active/publications/discussion_papers/dp.php?dpno=9358. [18]

Duffie, D. (2020), "Redesigning the US Treasury Market After the COVID19 Crisis", *Hutchins Center Working Paper*, Vol. June 2020/Number 62, https://www.brookings.edu/wp-content/uploads/2020/05/WP62_Duffie_v2.pdf. [20]

Fleming, M. (2020), "Treasury Market Liquidity and the Federal Reserve during the COVID-19 Pandemic", *Liberty Street Economics*, https://libertystreeteconomics.newyorkfed.org/2020/05/treasury-market-liquidity-and-the-federal-reserve-during-the-covid-19-pandemic.html. [16]

German Finanzagentur (2020), "Issues planned by the Federal government in the second quarter of 2020", *Press release*, Vol. April, https://www.deutsche-finanzagentur.de/fileadmin/user_upload/pressemeldungen/en/2020/2020-03-23_pm01_EK_Q2_en.pdf. [10]

Maravalle, A. and Ł. Rawdanowicz (2018), "To shorten or to lengthen? Public debt management in the low interest rate environment", *OECD Economics Department Working Papers*, No. 1483, OECD Publishing, Paris, https://dx.doi.org/10.1787/192ef3ad-en. [5]

OECD (2020), "OECD Economic Outlook", Vol. Volume 2020 Issue 2, https://doi.org/10.1787/39a88ab1-en. [1]

OECD (2020), *OECD Economic Outlook, Volume 2020 Issue 1*, OECD Publishing, Paris, https://dx.doi.org/10.1787/0d1d1e2e-en. [11]

OECD (2020), "OECD Pensions Outlook 2020", https://doi.org/10.1787/67ede41b-en. [4]

OECD (2020), "Sovereign Borrowing Outlook", Vol. Special COVID-19 Edition, https://doi.org/10.1787/dc0b6ada-en. [2]

OECD (2019), *OECD Sovereign Borrowing Outlook 2019*, OECD Publishing, Paris, https://dx.doi.org/10.1787/aa7aad38-en. [3]

OECD (2018), "Sovereign Borrowing Outlook", OECD Publishing, Paris, https://doi.org/10.1787/23060476. [9]

OECD (2014), *OECD Sovereign Borrowing Outlook 2014*, OECD Publishing, Paris, https://dx.doi.org/10.1787/sov_b_outlk-2014-en. [12]

Priftis, R. and S. Zimic (2021), "Sources of Borrowing and Fiscal Multipliers", *The Economic Journal*, Vol. Volume 131/Issue 633, pp. Pages 498–519, https://doi.org/10.1093/ej/ueaa051. [7]

The UK DMO (2020), "Official Operations in the Gilt Market", *Operational Notice*, https://www.dmo.gov.uk/media/16394/opnot060420.pdf. [8]

UK DMO (2020), "Response to an enquiry by Chairman of the Treasury Select Committee", https://committees.parliament.uk/publications/4108/documents/40708/default/. [13]

US Treasury (November 4, 2020), "Minutes of the Meeting of the Treasury Borrowing Advisory Committee of the Securities Industry and Financial Markets Association", https://home.treasury.gov/policy-issues/financing-the-government/quarterly-refunding/most-recent-quarterly-refunding-documents. [15]

Zhou, J. and P. Mauro (2020), "r-g<0: Can We Sleep More Soundly?", *IMF Working Paper* WP/20/52, https://www.imf.org/en/Publications/WP/Issues/2020/03/13/r-minus-g-negative-Can-We-Sleep-More-Soundly-49068. [17]

Annex 1.A. Methods and sources

Definitions and concepts used in the Sovereign Borrowing Outlook Survey

The Borrowing Outlook survey collects gross borrowing requirements, redemption and outstanding debt amounts with breakdown of these items by maturity, currency and interest rate types. It uses core definition of sovereign debt, so-called central government marketable debt, mainly due to its comparability and collectability. This measure, directly linked to the central government budget financing, enabled the OECD to collect not only for realisations but also for estimates of government borrowing requirements, funding strategies as well as outstanding debt with instruments, maturity and currency types.

Coverage of institutions: Central government

The coverage of institutions by debt statistics varies from public sector to central government. Public sector stands as broadest institutional coverage, as it includes local governments, state funds financial and non-financial public corporations as well as central government debt. General government definition, which is used by for example by OECD System of National Accounts (SNA), consists of central government, state and local governments and social security funds controlled by these units. Central government covers all departments, offices, establishments and other bodies classified under general government, which are agencies or instrument of the central authority of a country, except separately organised social security funds or extra-budgetary funds. In terms of layers of coverage of institutions, central government stands out as the core definition. Debt of central government is raised, managed and retired by the national DMOs on behalf of the central government. Hence, advantage of this relatively narrow definition of debt is that it enables countries to provide comparable figures, in particular for the estimations.

Coverage of types of debt: Marketable debt

In terms of instruments, liabilities can be in the form of debt securities, loans, insurance, pensions and standardised guarantee schemes, currency and deposits, and other accounts payable. Debt items can be classified as marketable and non-marketable debt. While marketable debt is defined as financial securities and instruments that can be bought and sold in the secondary market, non-marketable debt is not transferable. For example, bonds and bills issued in capital markets are marketable debt; multilateral and bilateral loans from the official sector are non-marketable debt.

The Borrowing Outlook survey focuses on marketable debt instruments, while most government debt statistics (e.g. OECD SNA, EU Maastricht debt, and IMF Public Sector Debt Statistics) cover both marketable and non-marketable debt items. OECD governments are financed predominantly by marketable debt instruments. This is a central definition for every analysis concerning various issues around debt management including borrowing conditions, portfolio composition, investor preferences and market liquidity. An advantage of using this definition is to indicate to investors which instruments are available for trade in the secondary market and which are not. Another reason is for the issuer to calculate different characteristics of the debt, such as duration or time to maturity, which in the case of non-marketable debt would present a difficult issue.

Terminology

- *Standardised Gross borrowing requirement* (GBR) for a year is equal to net borrowing requirement during that year plus the short-term redemptions on the capital market at the beginning of the same year. Also, the (estimated) cash balance may affect the funding needs. In other words, the size of

GBR in calendar year amounts to how much the DMO needs to issue in nominal terms so as to fully pay back maturing debt plus the net cash borrowing requirement through any issuance mechanism.

- *Net* borrowing *requirement (NBR)* is the amount to be raised for current budget deficit. While refinancing of redemptions is a matter of rolling over the same exposure as before, NBR refers to new exposure in the market.

- *The* funding *strategy* involves the choice of i) money market instruments for financing short-term GBR and ii) capital market instruments for funding long-term GBR. The strategy entails information on how borrowing needs are going to be financed using different instruments such as long-term, short-term, nominal, variable-rate, indexed bonds and FX-denominated debt.

- Gross *debt* corresponds to the outstanding debt issuance at the end of calendar years. This measure does not take the valuation effects from inflation and exchange rate movements, thus it is equal to the total nominal amount that needs to be paid back to the holders of the debt.

- Redemptions refers to the total amount of the principal repayments of the corresponding debt including the principal payments paid through buy-back operations in a calendar year.

Regional aggregates

- Total OECD area denotes the following 37 countries: Australia, Austria, Belgium, Canada, Chile, Colombia, Czech Republic, Denmark, Estonia, Finland, France, Germany, Greece, Hungary, Iceland, Ireland, Israel, Italy, Japan, Korea, Latvia, Lithuania, Luxembourg, Mexico, Netherlands, New Zealand, Norway, Poland, Portugal, Slovak Republic, Slovenia, Spain, Sweden, Switzerland, Turkey, the United Kingdom and the United States.

- The G7 includes seven countries: Canada, France, Germany, Italy, Japan, United Kingdom and the United States.

- The OECD euro area includes 17 members: Austria, Belgium, Estonia, Finland, France, Germany, Greece, Ireland, Italy, Latvia, Lithuania, Luxembourg, Netherlands, Portugal, Slovak Republic, Slovenia and Spain.

- In this publication, the Emerging OECD group (i.e. OECD emerging-market economies) is defined as including six countries: Chile, Colombia, Hungary, Mexico, Poland and Turkey.

- The euro (€) is the official currency of 19 out of 28 EU member countries. These countries are collectively known as the euro area. The euro area countries are Austria, Belgium, Cyprus, Estonia, Finland, France, Germany, Greece, Ireland, Italy, Latvia, Lithuania, Luxembourg, Malta, the Netherlands, Portugal, Slovakia, Slovenia, and Spain.

Calculations and data sources

- Estimates that are presented as a percentage of GDP are calculated using nominal GDP data from the *OECD Economic Outlook,* December 2020.

- Debt is measured as the face value of current outstanding central government debt. Face value, the undiscounted amount of principal to be repaid, does not change except when there is a new issue of an existing instrument. This coincides with the original promise (and therefore contractual obligation) of the issuer. DMOs often use face value when they report how much nominal debt will mature in future periods. One important reason for using face value is that it is the standard market practice for quoting and trading specific volumes of a particular instrument.

- To facilitate comparisons with previous versions of the Outlook, figures are converted into US dollars using exchange rates from 1 December 2009, unless indicated otherwise. Where currency are converted into US dollars using flexible exchange rates, notes in figures and tables refer explicitly to that approach. Source: Refinitiv. The effects of using alternative exchange rate assumptions (in particular, fixing the exchange rate versus using flexible exchange rates) are illustrated in Figures 1.3 and 1.4 of Chapter 1 of the *Sovereign Borrowing Outlook, 2016*.

- All figures refer to calendar years unless specified otherwise.
- Aggregate figures for gross borrowing requirements (GBR), net borrowing requirements (NBR), central government marketable debt, redemptions, and debt maturing are compiled from answers to the Borrowing Survey. The OECD Secretariat inserted its own estimates/projections in cases of missing information for 2020 and/or 2021, using publicly available official information on redemptions and central government budget balances.
- Yield group debt calculations in Figure 1.6 are based on all issuances and re-openings of fixed-rate bonds (i.e. data excludes: short-term instruments, indexed linked, floating rate instruments and strips). Data is sourced from Refinitiv.
- For Figure 1.7: Several central banks have become dominant holders of domestic government bonds. For the euro area countries, cumulative net purchases of government bonds in the Eurosystem Public Sector Purchase Programme and the Pandemic Emergency Purchase Programme at book value as of end-December.

Average term to maturity

The following notes were provided by countries in relation to their calculations of average term to maturity.

Annex Table 1.A.1. Average term to maturity country comments

Country	Note
Australia	Weighted average term to maturity calculation includes Treasury Bonds, Treasury Indexed Bonds and Treasury Notes. Security weightings are based on the face value of each instrument.
Chile	All marketable debt in Chile corresponds to Bonds. All calculation as of December 31st of each year. Some of them consider amortization with maturity January, 1st of the following year
Colombia	All marketable debt in Colombia corresponds to domestic bonds (TES) and foreign bonds.
Czech Republic	Marketable central government debt excludes savings government bonds (retail bonds).
Denmark	Excludes effects from swaps and other derivatives.
Estonia	Includes central government marketable debt only, excludes other levels of government.
France	Excludes swap effects
Germany	excludes swap effects and own holdings, maturities of inflation-linked securities are weighted by 0.75 %
Greece	The above-mentioned data refer to Long Term marketable debt securities (more than 1 year original maturity) and exclude Treasury Bills.
Hungary	Data excludes retail securities, locally issued FX bonds, loans, a non-marketable bond series held by the National Bank of Hungary (only negligible amount) and since 2020 also excludes the non-marketable bonds issued to municipalities. Data includes cross-currency swaps.
Iceland	Excludes swap effects.
Ireland	The estimated ATM for Ireland reflects bonds, Euro Commercial paper and Irish Treasury Bills. Inflation linked bonds and some ultra-long maturity notes issued since 2016 are excluded on the basis that they were issued as private placements. The total o/s for these products at end-2020 stood at €2.9bn, 2% of the total marketable debt o/s.
Israel	Estimated ATM excludes retail bonds and non-tradable bonds for pension funds and insurance companies
Italy	No security has been excluded; swap effects are excluded.
Japan	MOF announces ATM based on Fiscal Year, not Calendar Year. Figures from 2007 to 2019 exclude saving bonds. Figures of 2020 are estimated and include saving bonds.
Mexico	Our calculation of the ATM considers all outstanding market debt of the central government (short-term and long-term).
	Preliminary figures for 2020.

Country	Note
Netherlands	The information in the table is based on the data of Tbill and Bonds.
New Zealand	The calculation is based on all NZ government marketable securities including Nominal Bonds, Inflation-Indexed Bonds, and Treasury Bills. The calculation excludes the non-market securities held by NZ Reserve bank and Earthquake Commission. However, it includes securities held by the NZ Reserve bank that were purchased under their Large Scale Asset Purchase programme and Government Bond repurchases.
Norway	Includes all outstanding Treasury bills and government bonds
Portugal	Excludes securities issued for collateral purposes.
Spain	Central Government Treasury Bills, Bonds and Obligaciones (nominal, inflation linked and assumed) and foreign currency debt.
Sweden	Marketable debt securities include:
	Government bonds
	Inflation-linked bonds
	Green bonds
	Public bonds in foreign currencies
	Treasury bills
	Commercial paper, foreign currencies
Switzerland	Outstanding marketable debt, excluding:
	- own tranches not yet issued
	- securities for cash management purposes
	- swap effects
Turkey	Weighted average term to maturity (ATM) figures reflects central government marketable debt.
United Kingdom	Treasury bills for cash management purposes, DMO's gilt holdings and undated gilts are excluded from the calculation of the weighted average term to maturity.

Source: 2020 Survey on Central Government Marketable Debt and Borrowing.

Notes

[1] Net borrowing requirements are estimated to be higher than budget deficits in 2020. This may stem from various factors including governments' prefunding operations or financing of off-budget measures, as well as some new borrowing needs may not be reflected on budget deficit estimations.

[2] While this report was being prepared in January 2021, new financial packages were announced in a few countries including the US, exact size of which is not certain yet.

[3] The OECD economy is estimated to have contracted by 5.5% in 2020, with declines over 10% in few OECD countries (OECD, 2020[1]).

[4] The primary balance is defined as the overall fiscal balance excluding net interest payments on public debt. The primary balance, as one critical indicator of short-term sustainability, shows the extent to which governments can honour their debt obligations without the need for further indebtedness.

[5] Borrowing instruments –often in form of securities in the OECD area- include a wide range of options with different maturity, interest rate and currency characteristics. Securities can be sold through different methods including auctions, syndications, private placements and taps.

[6] It should be noted that when this report was finished in early February 2021, the yield on the benchmark US 10-year bond was hovering around 1.2%, amid the expectations of a large stimulus package to be enacted.

[7] Issuers of negative yielding debt have received premiums from these issues. An examination of negative yielding fixed-rate sovereign bond issuance in 17 OECD countries between 2014 and 2019 indicates that the volume of negative-yielding fixed-rate bond issues reached USD 3.6 trillion and issuers received more than USD 28 billion from these issues (https://dx.doi.org/10.1787/0d1d1e2e-en).

[8] At the beginning of the COVID-19 outbreak, risk aversion in financial markets rose substantially, and as investors' preference shifted towards cash (and cash-like instruments), selling pressure put strains on primary dealers' balance sheets. Please find detailed discussion concerning the turmoil in March 2020 in 2020 edition of the OECD Sovereign Borrowing Outlook.

[9] As widely discussed in the literature, rising risk premia and interest rates cause endogenous debt accumulation, which in turn deteriorates borrowing conditions (Corsetti and Dedola, 2013[18]) (Cohen and Villemot, 2011[19]).

[10] Under the SURE instrument, the European Council approved a total of Euro 90.3 billion in financial support to 18 Member States. Between October and December 2020, the European Commission issued USD 53.5 billion bonds in four rounds at very low yields. The issuance consisted of 5-, 10- and 15-year maturities bonds (https://ec.europa.eu/info/business-economy-euro/economic-and-fiscal-policy-coordination/financial-assistance-eu/funding-mechanisms-and-facilities/sure_en).

[11] Another example of contingency option for managing cash flows came from the United Kingdom, where the Bank of England has temporarily extended the use of the government's 'Ways and Means (W&M) facility' to manage liquidity and the short-term volatility of cash forecasts. The government usually uses this facility to finance its dayto- day spending, before the BoEs sells government bonds to the market. This facility is normally capped at GBP 370 million. See press releases from HM Treasury here, and BoE here.

2 Revisiting sovereign refinancing risk in light of COVID-19 crisis

Sovereign refinancing risk is attracting more attention due to the impact of the COVID-19 shock on sovereign borrowing needs. The surge in government borrowings to finance COVID-19 stimulus and related bailout packages throughout 2020 mechanically increased the outstanding debt that must be refinanced in the future.

While most governments in the OECD area today are paying very little interest to new borrowings across all maturities, the risk associated with the refinancing of debt at substantially higher rates is more of a medium- and long-term concern for most countries and a potential a short-term concern for at least some countries. Against this backdrop and from the perspective of a public debt manager, this chapter discusses how to identify measure and mitigate refinancing risk in light of possible scenarios as well as country experiences.

2.1. Introduction

What if existing debt needs to be refinanced at considerably higher interest rates in the future or, in the worst-case scenario, what if it cannot be rolled over at all? This is a key question for sovereigns who wish to manage their debt portfolio prudently. As the COVID-19 shock exemplified in 2020, various factors from market turbulence to a sudden increase in government borrowing needs can elevate the perception of sovereign refinancing risk. When realised, the refinancing risk may not only complicate government debt management, but also threaten a country's credibility and financial stability.

What are the key factors affecting vulnerability to refinancing risk? Why do some countries with high debt levels seem to be less vulnerable than others? Would high average maturity be sufficient to address the risk? What are the means of managing refinancing risk? This chapter addresses these questions by examining risk management techniques, including the role of building flexibility, and provides theoretical and practical examples.

Key findings

- Perceived sovereign refinancing risk reflects a confluence of factors including macroeconomic fundamentals, the degree of development of the domestic debt market, access to contingency funding tools as well as the size and composition of the outstanding debt stock. The perceived safety of debt is relatively higher in countries with stronger macroeconomic fundamentals, financial and political stability and access to liquid markets.

- Refinancing risk for a given country is considered elevated – ceteris paribus – when refinancing needs are high and the maturity profile of debt is short and/or is concentrated on or around a particular period.

- The upsurge in debt issuance by OECD governments in the wake of the COVID-19 crisis has mechanically increased the absolute amount of debt to be repaid or refinanced in the future. In tandem, the average maturity of sovereign borrowing, particularly at the initial stage of the crisis, has shortened considerably, as much of the additional cash needed by governments was financed through short-term debt.

- To better identify refinancing risk, common indicators such as average time-to-maturity, rollover ratios and interest re-fixing share of the debt should be complemented by a detailed examination of the debt redemption profile for redemption peaks.

- From a debt management perspective, the existing refinancing risk of a debt portfolio is managed strategically through new debt issuance and liability management operations such as outright buyback and switch operations.

- In terms of portfolio design for the future, use of simulation models such as 'Cost-at-Risk' can help sovereign issuers to assess the potential impact of borrowing strategies with different maturity and interest rate compositions. Judgements will need to be made to supplement the modelling results.

- A key element in managing refinancing risk, especially in view of the uncertain global outlook and increased refinancing needs, is building flexibility into sovereign financing programmes through contingency tools such as building up liquidity buffers, establishing credit lines and ensuring access to money markets.

- Timely and accurate communication of financing needs to investors is likely to reduce uncertainty, leading to more credible debt management and lower borrowing costs. In the wake of the COVID-19 crisis, sovereign issuers can benefit from fine-tuning their investor relations programmes with more frequent communication and effective use of digital communication tools.

2.2. Sovereign refinancing risk

In addition to financing budget deficits, sovereign debt management offices are in charge of refinancing previously issued debt, unless it is amortised. Even in the case of a balanced budget, principal redemptions will generally be funded by new issuance, that is, by rolling over debt. When a bond matures, the borrower's refinancing cost is affected by interest rate levels and credit market conditions at that time. In debt management, "refinancing or rollover risk" refers to situations in which debt may have to be rolled over at an unusually high interest cost or in which debt cannot be rolled over at all.

More broadly, refinancing risk is being comprised of two slightly separate parts: repricing or "re-fixing" risk and rollover risk. In this respect, managing refinancing risk is also about managing the risk between debt and cash management, with the latter carrying an imperative (i.e. meeting all payments as they come due) that does not apply to debt management (which is more about making active decisions with different options).

Refinancing risk is closely interlinked with interest rate risk (risk premia), as investors demand to be compensated for greater uncertainty. The greater the perceived refinancing risk, the higher the risk premiums on sovereign debt. It should be noted that the distinction between interest-rate risk and refinancing risk may be less pronounced in countries with stable macroeconomic conditions and well-developed markets.

The analysis of refinancing risk also contains useful information for debt sustainability analysis and, *vice versa*, in terms of forming a view of how current liabilities are likely to evolve over time. Clearly, debt sustainability is a broader concept that involves fiscal policy, so as to ensure prudent debt levels via government expenditures and taxes.[1] Granular analysis of refinancing risk and debt rollover cost are an integral part of debt sustainability analysis. Then again, if investors perceived a risk to debt sustainability, they would demand a higher risk premium for their investment (i.e. higher interest rates) which in turn increases the cost of debt refinancing.

2.2.1. Assessment of sovereign refinancing risk

When sovereign refinancing risk is perceived as high by investors, it is likely to create a circumstance where investors become reluctant to buy longer-term government bonds as these involve more lengthy exposure to the issuer and higher price risk to exit. Instead, they may limit themselves to investing in (very) short-term debt, thereby making the debt portfolio even more vulnerable. Given the scale of debt operations, heightened concerns about refinancing risk may not only make government debt management more challenging, but also threaten financial stability in a country. Economic literature presents abundant evidence of self-fulfilling debt crises, in particular in emerging countries (Cole and Kehoe, 2000[1]) (Arellano and Ramanarayanan, 2012[2]). Against this backdrop, proper assessment, management and communication of refinancing risk are of paramount importance to sovereign issuers.

In general, refinancing risk is more pronounced when refinancing needs are high, when the debt is denominated in foreign currency, and when the maturity profile of debt is short and/or is concentrated on or around a particular period.[2] As discussed in Section 2.4, a number of indicators can be used to measure and assess sovereign refinancing risk including average time-to-maturity, rollover ratio and maturity profile. While these indicators provide important insights into the assessment of refinancing risk, there are other factors affecting a sovereign's exposure to refinancing risk through liquidity and perceived safety of debt. A country can have the longest average maturity in the world but unless government is confident of meeting its debt obligation on maturity, it may not be of much use. Greece, for example, was one of the countries with the longest average maturity of its debt portfolio before the 2008 financial crisis. Conversely, a country with a relatively low average maturity may be perceived as less vulnerable to refinancing risk in view of other factors. For example, the United States has an average maturity of about 5 years, which was lower than the OECD average of 7.7 years in 2020. Yet, the United States is among the countries with the lowest perceived refinancing risk, largely due to its strong macroeconomic fundamentals, high credit ratings and access to the most liquid government securities markets.

The perceived safety of debt is relatively lower in countries that are characterised by volatile market conditions, rapidly deteriorating economic indicators, lower credit ratings, perception of poor governance, high political risk, high indebtedness, and financial distress (Jonasson and Papaioannou, 2018[3]). The ability to refinance debt at reasonable cost and desirable maturity requires, above all, a well-functioning, stable and liquid local currency bond market. Countries that can issue domestic currency debt generally face much lower refinancing risk, particularly for very short-term (T-bills) that are accepted as collateral by the domestic central bank. In the OECD area, for example, governments predominantly finance their budget deficits through local currency denominated debt. Local currency share of total central government marketable debt in the OECD area was about 95% as of 2020. Countries with shallow domestic debt markets or constrained market access, on the other hand, are often more vulnerable to changes in market conditions than mature market countries. In the wake of the COVID-19 shock, for example, investor concerns over sovereign refinancing risk in emerging market economies have heightened in view of pre-existing vulnerabilities. As discussed in Chapter 3, some countries lacking deep and liquid local currency bond markets, have faced serious financing challenges as their access to international capital markets impaired significantly, in particular at the initial stage of the COVID-19 crisis. Lacking the resources and borrowing capacity of advanced economies, the countries with heavy debt burdens have benefited from international efforts to avoid a liquidity crisis (i.e. financial support from IMF and World Bank, and G20 Debt Service Suspension Initiative).

A reliable and broadly diversified investor base is important for refinancing risk assessment as it supports stability and liquidity in government securities markets. Central banks and other institutional investors such as pension funds that give priority to credit quality and liquidity, and are less sensitive to interest rate developments, are considered to be stable investors. In this respect, several advanced economies such as Australia, Japan and the United States are viewed as countries with a particularly solid investor base (Arslanalp and Tsuda, 2014[4]). Conversely, heavy reliance on foreign investors (in particular foreign nonbank investors) in relatively small countries is associated with higher refinancing risk, as sovereign exposure to sudden investor outflows can obstruct the refinancing of debt. While of great importance for developing or maintaining liquid local bond markets, the share of the yield sensitive to foreign investors in an investor base requires careful consideration due to the risk of sudden investor outflow.[3]

It should be noted that in most cases, maturity composition of the debt issuance is also determined by investor preferences and market trends. For example, usually central banks, having conservative investment strategies, prefer short-dated securities for reserve management purposes, while institutional investors such as insurance companies and pension funds invest in long-term bonds to match the maturity of their liabilities. Strong demand for long-term assets from pension funds in the United Kingdom, and life insurance companies in Japan enable respective sovereign debt management offices (DMOs) to sell super long-term bonds (i.e. bonds with a 30-year maturity or more).[4] Irrespective of the fiscal outlook in these countries, the cost of refinancing existing debt has remained low amid high liquidity and perceived safety of debt in part thanks to their stable investor base.

One of the major shifts in the investor base in advanced economies in recent years has been the greater role of domestic central banks in government bond markets. Even before the pandemic, central banks became the dominant holders of government bonds in several countries as a result of the quantitative easing policies launched by major central banks.[5] In the wake of the COVID-19 crisis, central bank purchases that sought to restore smooth market functioning and support inflation and or economic objectives have had an impact on the market perception of sovereign refinancing risk. Increased net government bond purchases by major central banks have helped to absorb increased supply and eased interest rate risk for their countries by keeping borrowing costs very low at least over the near future.

2.3. Impact of the epidemic on sovereign refinancing needs in the OECD area

The COVID-19 crisis has taken a heavy toll on public finances across the OECD area. As presented in Chapter 1, the gross borrowings of OECD governments from the markets are expected to jump 60% to USD18 trillion in 2020. As a result of the upsurge in debt issuance, the outstanding level of central government debt securities is estimated to have risen to USD 55 trillion by the end of 2020 (see Chapter 1 for more information). Hence, the absolute amount of debt to be repaid or refinanced in the future has reached an unprecedented level. Figure 2.1 illustrates central government marketable debt redemption projections as a percentage of outstanding debt in the OECD area between 2022 and 2031. The overall debt redemption profile is projected to decrease gradually over time, although redemptions will be relatively high in 2025 and 2030, largely due to the increase in 5- and 10-year benchmark bond issues in 2020.

Figure 2.1. Ten-year redemptions of central government marketable debt in OECD country groupings, as a percentage of debt stock

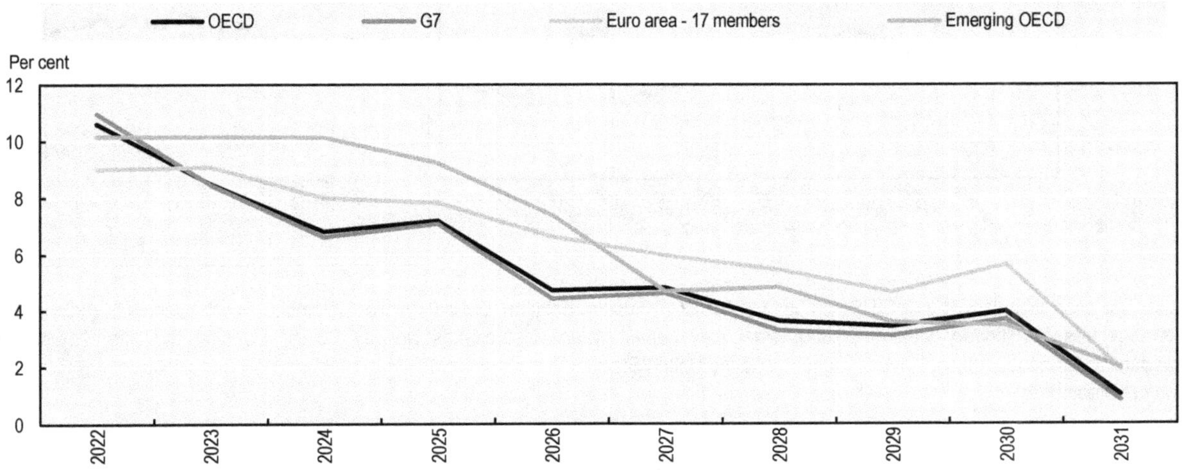

Note: Using the debt comparable application data, calculated on USD amounts outstanding as at 19 January 2021.
Source: OECD calculations based on data from Refinitiv.

The abrupt increase in borrowing needs has altered the maturity profile of debt issuance. In 2020, the average maturity of sovereign borrowing shortened considerably, as most of the additional cash needs of governments was financed through short-term debt (e.g. Treasury Bills and commercial paper). Chapter 1 offers a comprehensive assessment of the trends in terms of key indicators of refinancing risk. For example, the share of short-term instruments in central government marketable debt issuance in the OECD area increased from 40% in 2019 to 48% in 2020. Correspondingly, key indicators of refinancing risk exposure such as rollover ratio and average term-to-maturity (ATM) of outstanding debt worsened. As of January 2021, 25% of the outstanding amount of government securities is due in the next 12 months; and 45% is due in next 36 months. The resulting dynamics implies a general rise in sovereign refinancing risk.

Despite the unprecedented increased refinancing needs, interest rates on government securities have remained low, and even declined further in most OECD countries after a period of high turbulence in funding markets in March. Unlike the aftermath of both the 2008 financial crisis and the euro area sovereign debt crisis, this time around, OECD governments have not experienced major changes in their sovereign credit ratings, except for a few countries including Mexico, Turkey and the United Kingdom. Overall, risk spreads on sovereign bonds have remained stable in recent years, except for a few episodes of heightened volatility (e.g. December 2018, September 2019 and March 2020) (Figure 2.2). A major factor behind the benign risk assessments is medium-long term impact of the fiscal stimulus programmes on the economic growth. As economies are expected to recover on the back of expansionary monetary and fiscal policy, so as the debt repayment capacities.

Figure 2.2. 10-year CDS spreads

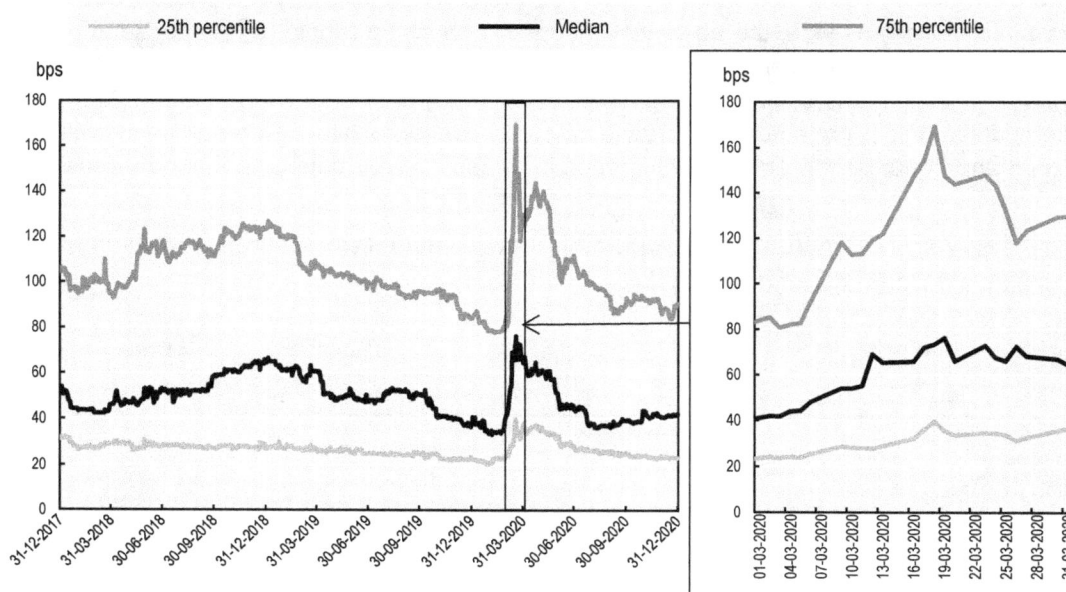

Note: The chart includes 10 year CDS spreads for Australia, Austria, Belgium, Canada, Chile, Colombia, Czech, Denmark, Finland, France, Germany, Greece, Hungary, Iceland, Ireland, Israel, Italy, Japan, Mexico, Netherlands, Norway, Poland, Portugal, Slovakia, Slovenia, Spain, Sweden, Switzerland, Turkey, United Kingdom, and the United States.
Source: Bloomberg.

To some extent, it can be argued that sovereign risk assessment currently benefits from the current low interest rate environment which is, in part, supported by the quantitative easing (QE) programmes of major central banks. The increased net purchases of government bonds by major central banks helped to absorb the steep increase in bond supply. In 2020, while net marketable debt issuance by OECD governments is estimated at USD 8.6 trillion, net purchases of government bonds by major central banks exceeded USD 4.5 trillion. At the same time, however, central banks have become the single largest creditors to their sovereigns in a number of countries, as they have been engaged in QE programmes since 2009, which were reinforced during the COVID-19 shock. Once the global economy is on firmer footing with higher inflation expectations, the outlook for monetary policy will need to shift, which may result in tapering/ withdrawing of some QE programmes. Tapering of QE programmes has important implications for financial markets in general, and for sovereign funding conditions in particular, mainly through changes in borrowing interest rates and the investor base. The impact of higher interest rates on the cost of debt would initially be relatively low in countries where new borrowing needs are limited and the share of fixed-rate debt with long maturity is high. In terms of the investor base, a lower level of involvement of central banks as large buyers should lead to increased funding needs from other investors such as commercial banks.

2.4. Measuring refinancing risk through key indicators

Among all the financial risks (refinancing risk, liquidity risk, market risk and credit risk), refinancing risk and short-term liquidity risk likely represent the most significant financial risk for sovereigns. For most countries, and particularly after the COVID-19 shock, in each calendar year there is a budget deficit, because government revenues are lower than the expenditures. The deficit for a calendar year is added to the debt redemption schedule constructed from previously accumulated budget deficits. The ability of a country to finance both the budget deficit and the debt maturing in a calendar year is crucial. A clear methodology to identify, measure and mitigate the refinancing risk is needed. This section presents the main indicators to measure the refinancing risk and, equally importantly, explains their limitations using theoretic examples.

2.4.1. Key indicators

Average Time to Maturity (ATM)

The most common indicator used to measure the refinancing risk is Average Time to Maturity (ATM). This indicator measures the weighted average time to maturity of all the principal payments in a debt portfolio. The higher this figure, the lower the refinancing risk because on average there is more time to repay the principal's payments. The Equation [1] in Box 2.1 presents the calculation of the ATM.

Rollover Ratio (ROR 1Y)

The rollover ratio for one year (ROR 1Y) measures the percentage of short-term debt up to one year divided by the total debt. The lower this ratio, the lower the refinancing risk. The added value of this indicator is a better understanding of the immediate financial needs which must be rolled over in that year. Equation [2] in Box 2.1 presents the calculation of the ROR for one year.

$$[2]\ RoR\ 1Y = \frac{R_1}{Total\ Debt}$$

Rollover Ratio (ROR 3Y)

For the purpose of having wider perspective of the refinancing risk, a complementary indicator is the rollover ratio for three years (ROR 3Y). This indicator measures the percentage of debt maturing in the next three years as a percentage of total debt. Similar to the rollover ratio for one year, the lower this ratio, the lower the debt maturing in the next three years and therefore the lower the refinancing risk. Equation [3] in Box 2.1 presents the calculation of the ROR for three years.

Box 2.1. Mathematical Equations

Equation [1] presents the calculation of the ATM:

$$[1]\ ATM = \frac{\sum_{t=1}^{n} R_t \times t}{Total\ Debt}$$

Where: ATM is the average time to maturity

- t is the time to maturity
- R_t is the amount of redemption in each year
- Total Debt is the total redemption calculated as $\sum_{t=1}^{n} R_t$

Equation [2] presents the calculation of the ROR for one year:

$$[2]\ ROR\ 1Y = \frac{R_1}{Total\ Debt}$$

Where: ROR 1Y is the rollover ratio for one year

- R_1 is the amount of redemption up to one year
- Total Debt is the total redemption calculated as $\sum_{t=1}^{n} R_t$

Equation [3] presents the calculation of the ROR for three years

$$[3] \; RoR \; 3Y = \frac{\sum_{t=1}^{3} R_t}{Total \; Debt}$$

Where: ROR 3Y is the rollover ratio for three years;

- t is the time to maturity
- R_t is the amount of redemption in each year
- Total Debt is the total redemption calculated as $\sum_{t=1}^{n} R_t$

2.4.2. Limitations of indicators

This section provides some stylised examples to demonstrate some misconceptions about refinancing risk and, in particular, how a simple reliance on ATM may be misleading.

Example 1: Consider three countries with total debt of 500 billion US dollars. Using Equation [1] the ATM for each country can be calculated. As shown in Figure 2.3 the ATM of country A is 11 years, country B is 8 years and for country C the ATM is 6 years. Based on this measurement, country A is the most prudent in terms of refinancing risk because it has the highest ATM.

Figure 2.3. Average term to maturities for three synthetic scenarios

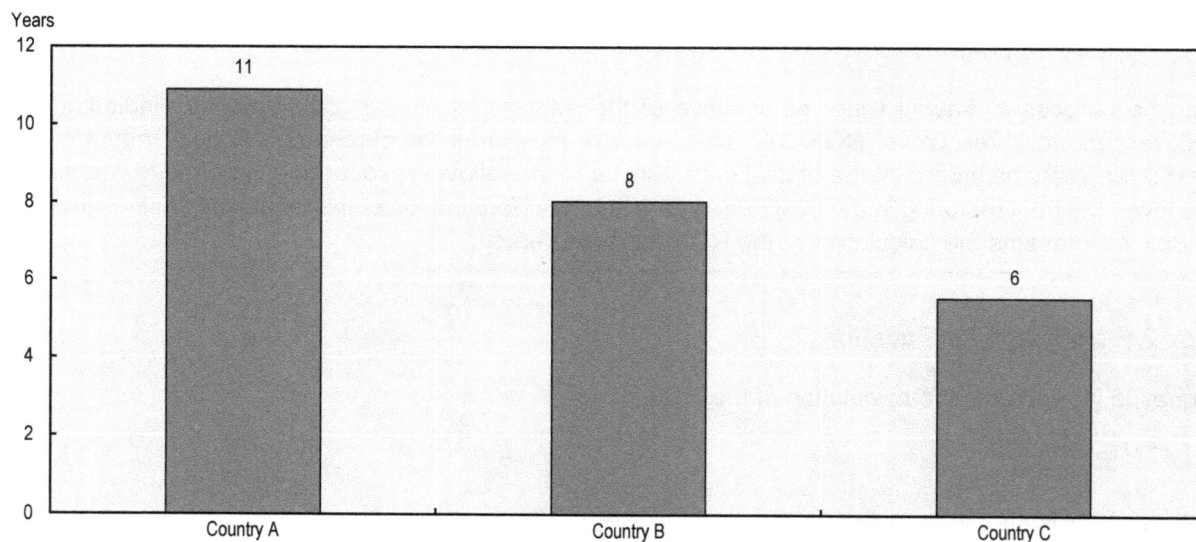

Note: This figure presents the average term to maturities for three theoretical scenarios. Each scenario denominated by a different country.
Source: Illustrative example.

Using Equation [2] and the debt redemption schedule of each country described in Figure 2.6, the rollover ratio for each country is presented in Figure 2.4. The rollover ratio of country A is $90\% = \frac{450}{500}$, while for country B it is $20\% = \frac{100}{500}$ and 30% for country C. Although the ATM of country A is the longest at 11 years, 90% of the debt is maturing in the next year which significantly increases the risk of failure to repay the debt. Therefore, based on the rollover ratio for one year country B is the most prudent for refinancing risk because it has the lowest rollover ratio.

Figure 2.4. Rollover ratio for one year for three synthetic scenarios

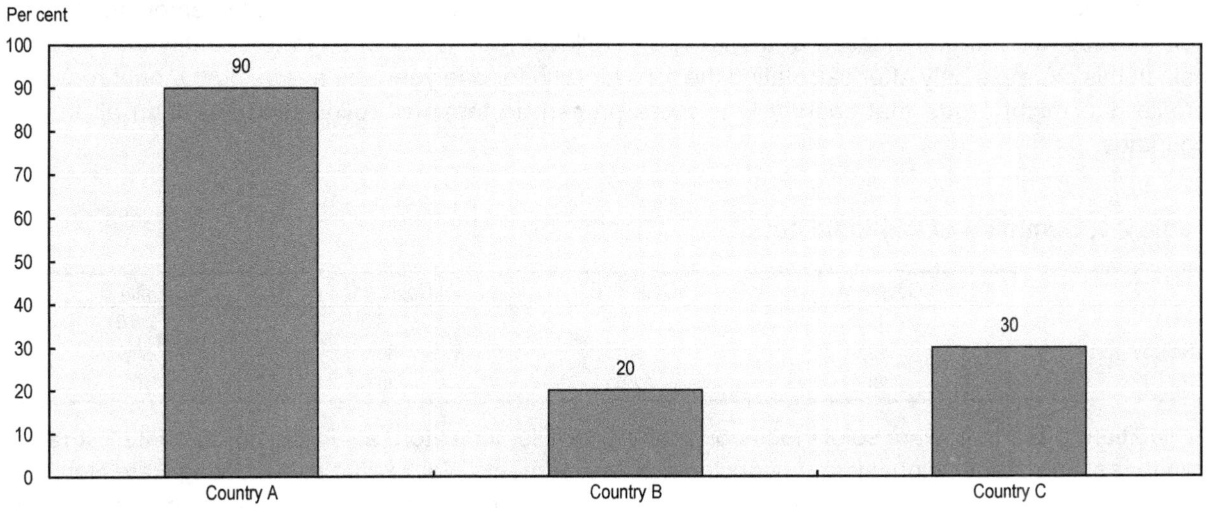

Note: This figure presents the rollover ratio for one year for three theoretical scenarios. Each scenario denominated by a different country.
Source: Illustrative example.

Then, using Equation [3] and the debt redemption schedule of each country described in Figure 2.6, the rollover ratio for three years of each country can be calculated. As shown in Figure 2.5, the rollover ratio of country A is $90\% = \frac{450}{500}$ while for country B it is $94\% = \frac{470}{500}$ and 30% for country C. Notwithstanding that these examples represent a somewhat more extreme situation than is usually the case, they reveal that although the rollover ratio of country B is the lowest, the redemption in the next three years is 94% of the debt. Taking under consideration this indicator suggests that country C is demonstrates lower refinancing risk.

Figure 2.5. Rollover ratio for three years for three synthetic scenarios

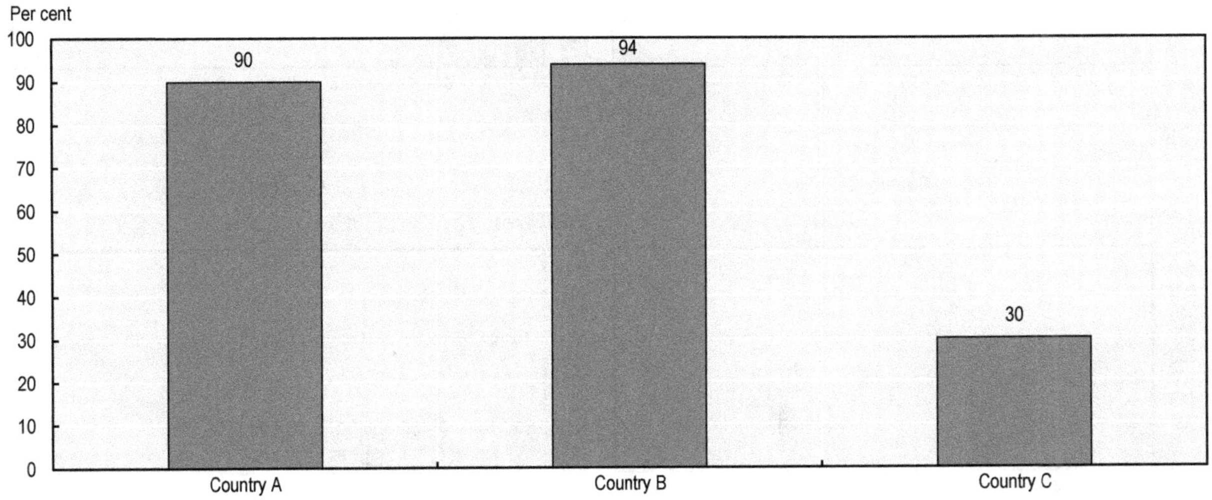

Note: This figure presents the rollover ratio for three year for three theoretical scenarios. Each scenario denominated by a different country.
Source: Illustrative example.

54 |

Example 2: Let's assume there is another country, country D. Applying Equation [1] and Equation [3] to the debt redemption scheduled described in in Figure 2.6, the ATM and the rollover ratio for three years calculations for country D yield identical figures to those of country D. This example demonstrates that, in some cases, even a combination of the ATM and rollover ratio is not enough to quantify the refinancing risk. In this example only after calculating the rollover ratio for one year and analysing the debt redemption profile one might argue that country D is more prudent in terms of refinancing risk than all the other countries.

Table 2.1. Summary of key indicators

	Country A	Country B	Country C	Country D
ATM	11.0	8.0	6.0	6.0
RoR 3Y	90%	94%	30%	30%
RoR 1Y	90%	20%	30%	10%

In addition to the indicators solely focus on maturity profile, indicators aiming to capture interest rate risk can reveal important insights into refinancing risk assessments. For example, a Floating Rate Note (FRN) can have a very long time to maturity when issued but has the same risk exposure to changes in short-term interest rates as a T-bill. In this respect, measuring 'interest rate composition' and 'time-to-Refixing' of a debt portfolio can shed additional light on the refinancing risk.[6]

Figure 2.6. Debt redemption schedule

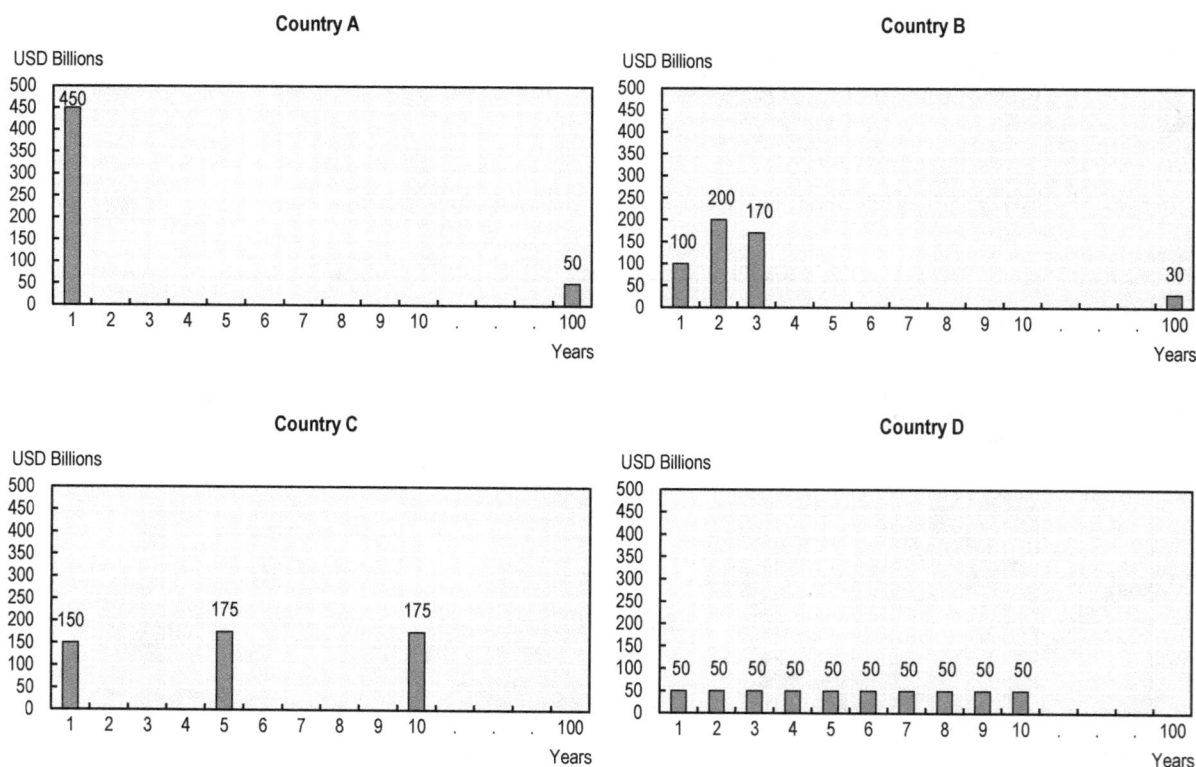

Note: This figure presents the debt redemption scheduled for three theoretical scenarios. Each scenario denominated by a different country.
Source: Illustrative example.

2.5. Means of managing refinancing risk

A comprehensive approach to managing refinancing risk combines the use of strategic design and contingency funding tools. The key point is to balance consistency in the funding strategy with sufficient flexibility in case of market disruption. While a theoretical model can be useful for representing a benchmark redemption profile with desired features, it may prove to be difficult, if not impossible, to achieve. Often sovereign debt managers design short, medium and long-term funding strategies by taking into account the profile of future redemptions. In this regard, analyses of expected cost and risk of alternative strategies through models can provide useful information to compare different borrowing scenarios. In addition, introducing pre-event contingency tools, such as credit lines with central banks or commercial banks and liquidity buffers along with post-event tools such as money market instruments, help to mitigate temporary cash shortfalls and reduce the refinancing risk.

2.5.1. Benchmark redemption profile of a theoretical model

One effective model for managing the refinancing risk is to plan the debt redemption profile according to a theoretical model based on a desired cost-risk trade-off. As described in the previous section, the debt redemption profile basically determines the key risk indicators, such as the ATM and rollover ratio of the debt portfolio. The model is based on the idea of maintaining the same redemption profile every year, which can be achieved by issuing fixed amount to the same benchmark term (see the example below). To illustrate the model, let's assume that the desired debt redemption profile for a debt stock of USD 670 billion is according to Figure 2.7. Key risk indicators for the refinancing risk can be calculated based on this example: Equation [1] on ATM yields 9.1 years; Equation [2] on rollover ratio for one year yields $13.4\% = \frac{90}{670}$ and; Equation [3] on the rollover ratio for three years yields $40.2\% = \frac{270}{670}$.

Figure 2.7. Debt redemption profile at year T

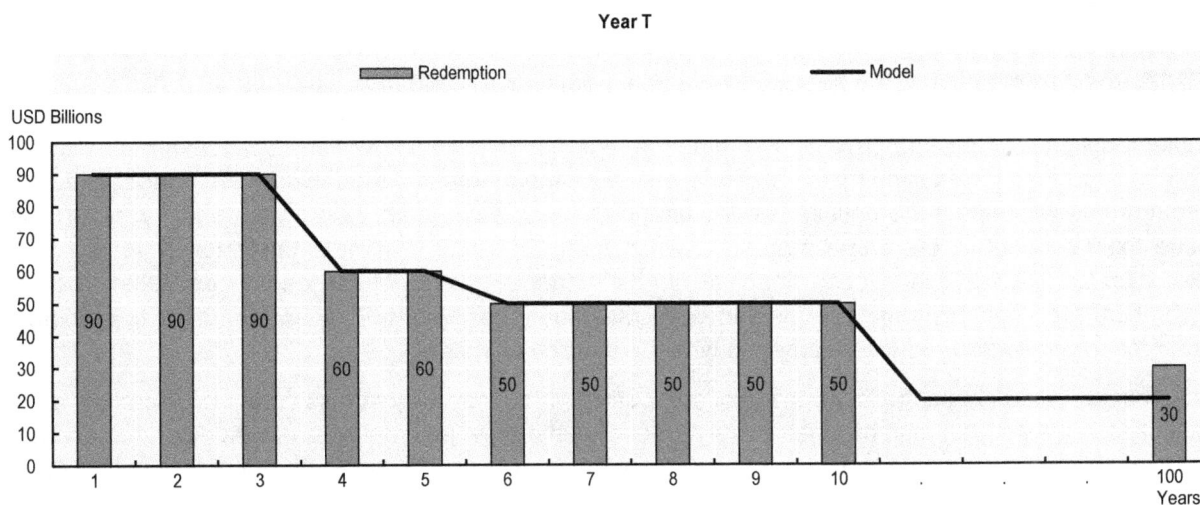

Source: Illustrative example.

For illustrative purposes, it is assumed that these indicators are consistent with the country risk appetite and issuer wishes to maintain this redemption profile next year. To do so, the first step is to understand that, in this example, the redemption profile is constructed by issuing three benchmarks (for simplicity, the benchmark for 100 years is ignored); 3 years, 5 years and 10 years. Hence, next year if the desire is to maintain the same redemption profile, i.e. 90 billion US dollars in the first, second and third year, 60 billion US dollars in year 4 and 5 and 50 billion US dollars in year 6 to 10, then the country should issue 30 billion US dollars for 3 years, 10 billion US dollars for 5 years and 50 billion US dollars for 10 years. As shown in Figure 2.8 after one year the same redemption profile will be maintained.

Figure 2.8. Debt redemption profile at year T+1

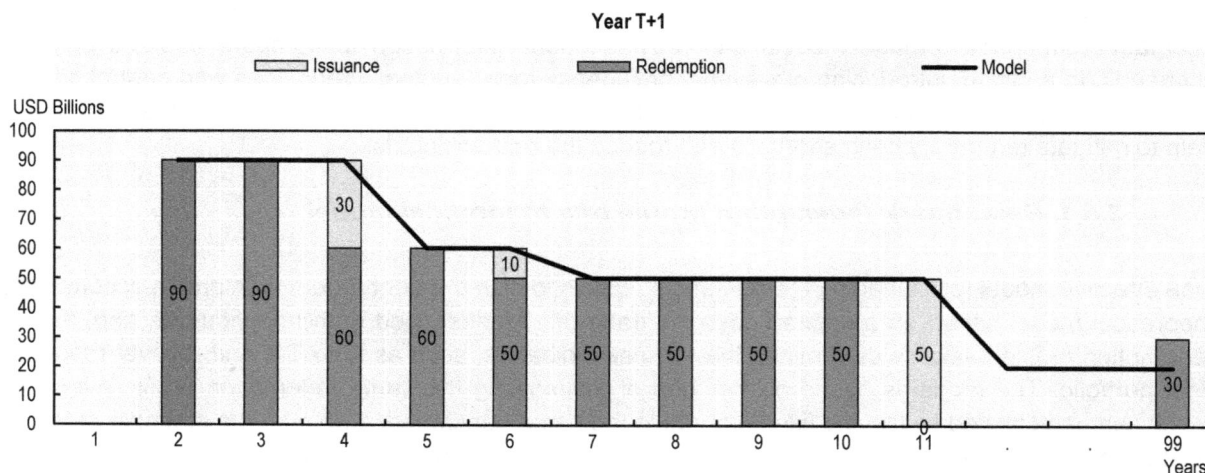

Source: Illustrative example.

The rollover ratio for one and three years will remain the same, while the ATM is to decrease from 9.1 years to 8.9 years due to the maturity of the ultra-bond reduced to 99 years (instead of 100).

While the idea is very simple, actually keeping the redemption profile consistent to the theoretical model each year is very complex. First and foremost, the basic principle of the model is to issue fixed amounts at the same maturities each year. However, the actual financial requirements, which determine the amount to issue, might vary considerably from one year to the other. As well known, the financial needs each year consist of the redemption in the next year and the current deficit. Therefore, if the current redemption profile is volatile between the years the financial needs will be very different each year. Of course after implementing the model consistently with time the redemption schedule will fit the model profile. However, even in case the current redemption profile is based on the theoretical model, different budget executions through time will impact dramatically on the financial needs each year, which will make it very difficult to issue fixed amount at the same maturities each year. One way to handle the volatility in the budget execution is to issue the excess financial needs (financial needs which lead to deviations from the theoretical redemption profile) for medium-long maturities, so there will be enough time to smooth the redemption profile and reduce divergence with the theoretical model.

The second major challenge is the investor's appetite, which may vary across time, and therefore make it difficult to issue according to the theoretical model. For instance, in times of stress investor demand tends to focus on short-term bonds, which makes issuance of long-term maturities difficult. For countries issuing Inflation Linked Bonds (ILBs), the level of inflation and inflation expectations impact on the demand for conventional bonds and ILBs, and therefore on the ability to smooth the redemption profile through time according to the planned redemption profile.

2.5.2. Strategic design of funding strategies with refinancing risk considerations

The profile of debt redemptions should be a key consideration when designing funding strategies, including setting the maximum amount that can be issued along the yield curve. Sovereign debt managers should seek to achieve a balance between the volume of debt due in each year and the monthly distribution of debt maturing within the individual years. Box 2.2. and 2.3 provide information on the experiences of Israeli and Italian debt management offices with financing risk modelling and implementation, respectively.

Models such as Cost-at-Risk can be used to assess alternative funding strategies from a cost at risk perspective as well as to optimise the interest rate risk strategy within certain constraints. Cost-at-Risk, which allows for quantification of risk in terms of the maximum costs that could occur with a given probability in a particular year, is one of the possible tools used to compare alternative debt structures. Implementing this approach requires first and foremost to define the policy objective. Usually, the main objective is to choose a financing strategy that minimizes the cost of debt, subject to certain risk appetite. Nevertheless, there could be another main objective and/or associated objectives, such as maintaining a well-functioning government bond market.

Second, debt managers should define how to measure cost and risk, which have a variety of dimensions. Firstly, cost and risk can be computed in absolute terms (i.e. billions of USD) or in relative terms such as a percentage of the outstanding debt stock or GDP, while the perspective of the calculation can be annual or cumulative (over the analysis horizon). Secondly, the measurement can be cost-related risk or budget-related risk. A key difference between the two approaches is the analysis horizon. While under the budget-related risk approach, the cost related risk refers to the fiscal year, the former approach take an intertemporal view when measuring the cost related risk. A useful measure for the cost is the debt service cost defined as the sum, in cash flow terms of the coupon payments over the analysis time horizon In turn, the measurement for the risk captures the uncertainty surrounding the debt-service cost. A common measurement is the volatility in the debt service cost measured using the standard deviation. Other measures evaluate the tail risk such as the upper 95th percentile of the debt service cost distribution. A less common approach is to measure the refinancing risk using indicators such as the rollover (measuring the amount of debt that matured in a given period) or refixing share of the debt.

Third, debt managers should choose the specification of the optimization model and particularly the stochastic procedures. The stochastic simulation assists in dealing with uncertainty of market key risks (such as interest rates, FX exposure and inflation rates), macro economy policy and the interrelationships between these factors. Model risk in debt strategy analysis can be reduced by using several specifications and by testing the robustness of the model to different parameters, assumptions and interactions of the variables.

Finally, one could run a wide range of financing strategies and calculate the cost-risk trade-off of each one and their ability to achieve the policy objective. In that regard it is important to mention that the objective of this model is not to choose one "optimal" financing strategy, but rather to illustrate the cost risk trade-off of different issuance strategies and to shed additional light on the refinancing risk. Furthermore, modelling outputs will need to be evaluated using careful judgements about the other salient factors behind the final choice of the debt strategy, including investor demand and primary market intermediation capacity, as well as any limitations of the model.

Box 2.2. Debt redemption model: The case of Israel

As described in detail in Section 2.5 and shown in Figure 2.9 the debt redemption profile is managed carefully according to a debt redemption model, which determines the key risk indicators, such as the Average Time to Maturity (ATM), rollover ratio for one and three years and the smoothness of the redemption profile. Other indicators such as the share of floating rate and the Average Time to Re-fixing (ATR) are also used to measure the refinancing risk. The ATM of the total debt is quite long standing at roughly 9.5 years, and the rollover ratio for one and three years is relative low standing on roughly 8% and 25% respectively. The level of these indicators depends on the risk appetite and the desired cost-risk trade-off. The ATR is 9.2 years and the share of floating rate as a percentage of the debt is roughly 4%.

Figure 2.9. Debt redemption profile (as of September 2020)

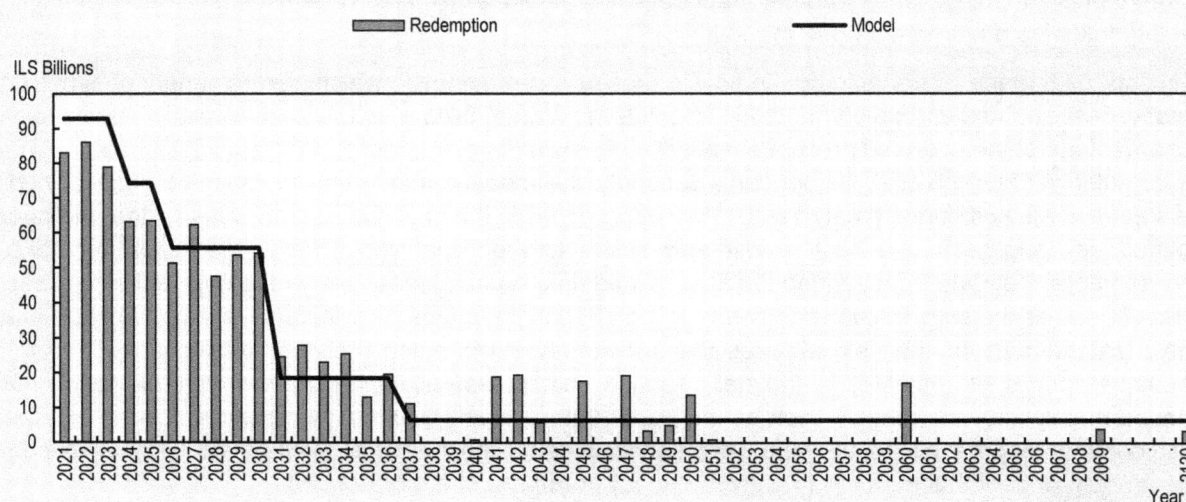

Note: This Figure presents the government debt redemption profile.
Source: Israel Government Debt Management Unit, Accountant General, Ministry of Finance.

The funding strategy is diversified between markets (domestic versus global) and instruments (conventional bonds, inflation-linked bonds and floating rate notes). In the domestic market, tradable benchmark bonds are issued for 1, 3, 5, 10 and 30 years. In 2020, a 20-year maturity bond was introduced due to the COVID-19 shock. In the global markets the steady state strategy is to issue once a year a benchmark size, usually dual-tranche rotating each year between US dollar and euros. For example, in January 2020 a dual-tranche benchmark issuance was executed for 10 and 30 years. However, due to the COVID-19 shock in March, a three-tranche, dollar-denominated issuance of USD 5 billion was executed for 10-years, 30-years and for the first time 100-years (century bond) and in April a USD 5 billion 40-year bond was issued in the Asian market. The ultra-long issuances increased the ATM dramatically but not necessarily the refinancing risk – at least not in the short-medium period. In addition, switch operations are implemented on a regular basis to manage the refinancing risk and to support other targets, such as enhancing liquidity in the secondary market. An additional flexible instrument which help to mitigate temporary cash shortfalls at low cost is Treasury bills. As shown in Figure 2.10, the issuance of Treasury bills was re-introduced in 2019 after declining consistently since the European sovereign debt crisis in 2011-2012. Due to COVID-19 the amount of Treasury bill issuances and switch auctions has increased significantly (roughly 80%).

Figure 2.10. Switch auctions and Treasury bill issuances (as of September 2020)

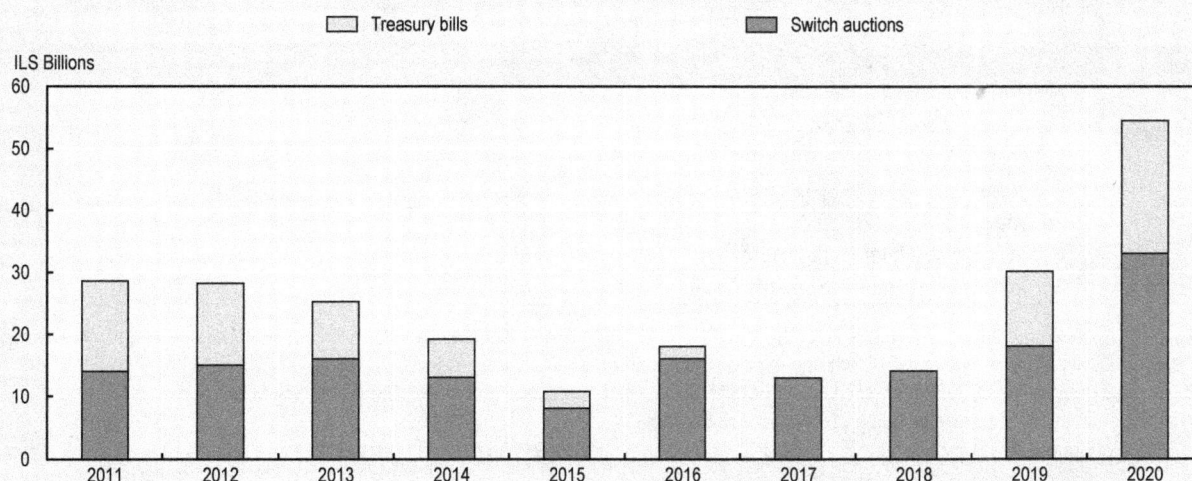

Note: This Figure presents the annual switch auctions and Treasury bill issuances since 2011. More information about the strategy to mitigate the refinancing risk is available at the annual and quarterly reports on the Israeli Ministry of Finance website. https://www.gov.il/BlobFolder/dynamiccollectorresultitem/annual-debt-reports-2019/en/annual-debt-report_YearsRepor_2019-en.pdf.
Source: Israel Government Debt Management unit, Accountant general, Ministry of Finance.

Box 2.3. 2018-20 review and implementation of the benchmark portfolio strategy – The case of Portugal

In 2018, IGCP pursued the reimplementation of the benchmark portfolio, aiming at providing a reference for public debt management. The project is aligned with the ultimate goal of minimizing the risk-adjusted cost of debt on a long-term horizon.

The benchmark portfolio rests on issues of Portuguese Government Bonds (PGB) according to a Benchmark Financing Strategy (BFS). In order to get the BFS, an efficient frontier of financing strategies was obtained from long-term simulations of economic (GDP and budget balances) and financial variables (interest rates), subject to specific market constraints and expert judgment. The BFS was selected from the efficient frontier as the strategy consisting of portfolio with the characteristics depicted in table 1. Metrics as ATM or WAM, modified duration and one-year to five-year rollover ratios were key for the selection of the optimal portfolio (as market constraints and expert judgement were incorporated in the modelling and selection stages by calibration of these variables) and later to assess the relative performance of the real portfolio.

In 2019 and 2020, the duration of the State's direct debt increased vis-à-vis the duration of the benchmark portfolio's debt against the backdrop of historically low interest rates and high demand for long-dated securities. As illustrated in Table 2.2, the modified duration of the State's direct debt at the end of 2020 stood 0.5 points above the benchmark's modified duration, whereas its cumulative cost (non-annualized) since the beginning of 2019 was only 0.4 percentage points higher. Not only did ATM and modified duration stand higher in the State Direct Debt portfolio than the benchmark, but the refinancing risk has also improved. Moreover, the risk-adjusted cost of the real portfolio was marginally lower than the one of the benchmark portfolio. Alternative cost indicators were computed, namely Cost at Risk, but the conclusions above were found unchanged.

Table 2.2. Cost and risk indicators at 31 December, 2020

	State Direct Debt portfolio	Benchmark portfolio
Average maturity (years)	7.0	6.5
Modified duration [1]	5.4	4.9
Percentage of debt refinancing:		
in 1 year	14.9%	17.6%
in 3 years	30.4%	33.1%
in 5 years	44.1%	51.1%
Accumulated cost from 31-12-2018 [2]	9.8%	9.4%
Accumulated cost / modified duration	1.8%	1.9%

Note: [1] The modified duration is a measure of the market value of debt with respect to changes in market interest rates; [2] The cost represents the internal rate of return (not annualized) and is calculated as the percentage change of the market value of debt between 31st December, 2018 and 31st December, 2020 after accounting for cash-flows within the period (dollar-weighted return). A fall in market interest rates will lead to an increase in the cost, all else being equal, and vice-versa.
Source: Portuguese Treasury and Debt Management Agency (Agência de Gestão da Tesouraria e da Dívida Pública - IGCP, E.P.E).

2.5.3. Bond switches and buybacks

Sovereign debt managers can use liability management operations, such as bond switches and buybacks, to attain a desired structure of debt portfolio. Bond switches (i.e. redeeming short-term bonds by issuing medium and long-term bonds) and buyback operations can help in reducing roll-over peaks in line with the desired redemption profile and thus lowering refinancing risk by reducing the outstanding amounts of bonds close to maturity.[7] While the aim is to reduce refinancing risk, cost considerations associated with a buyback premium and the benefit of lower funding costs through enhanced liquidity are generally analysed and factored in the overall cost-risk trade-off framework (Jonasson and Papaioannou, 2018[3]).

The use of bond buybacks and switches is a common practice among OECD sovereign debt management offices (DMOs). The 2020 OECD surveys of primary market developments and of liquidity in secondary government bond markets among DMOs revealed that more than 85% of OECD DMOs conduct either buyback or switch operations. There are different approaches to use of these tools in terms of methods (e.g. pricing), frequency and techniques (e.g. reverse auction and outright purchase, and use of sinking funds). For example, Italian DMO consider buyback as extraordinary operations and use a set of criteria to select bonds to be purchased back (Box 2.4). Some DMOs, like in France, Germany, Sweden and United Kingdom, carry out buyback operations on a regular basis via the secondary market (i.e. outright purchase). Some other DMOs like Portugal execute regular bond switches through auctions without a pre-defined calendar, using these operations as an opportunity to re-open off-the-run benchmarks and smooth the redemption profile.

There are several factors to be properly assessed when using buyback and switch facilities. For example, caution should be taken to assess the cost effectiveness of these operations, as buybacks of illiquid lines may crystalize illiquidity costs on the public sector's balance sheet. In addition, accounting effects of large buyback operations needs to be considered (e.g. impact on budget deficit and outstanding debt stock). In the case of switches, DMOs should also take into account investor demand for the issued securities and the efficiency of the yield curve.

Box 2.4. Use of buyback operations: The case of Italy

Buyback operations in Italy are considered as extraordinary operations, not subject to a fixed annual calendar. Operations are funded by cash surpluses and funds available from the Sinking Fund for Government bonds.

The criteria used by the Italian Treasury to select bonds to be purchased back are as follows. The first criterion is the shape of the redemption profile, whereby bonds that contribute to reimbursement peaks are bought back. The second criterion is liquidity, whereby the Treasury selects off-the-runs with the goal of avoiding a negative impact on secondary market liquidity. Moreover, in some circumstances, specific segments (i.e. inflation linked bonds, floater, etc.) can be chosen in order to re-establish an orderly market condition. The third criterion is the (potential) impact on outstanding debt. In order to smooth the public debt redemption profile, the Italian Treasury traditionally repurchases bonds with a residual maturity up to 18 months (taking into account market conditions). In order to have the maximum impact on the debt reduction, bonds with cash prices below par have major preference.

Buybacks in Italy can be conducted via a competitive (multi-price) auction or Treasury mandate, depending on the quantity to be bought back and market conditions.

2.5.4. Building flexibility in case of market disruption

As described in the previous section, there are real life challenges to theoretical models. In the event of a significant rise in interest rates and/or liquidity dry up in the financial market, having contingency funding tools, a diversified investor base and efficient communication with investors can be useful. Hence, a key element in managing the refinancing risk is building flexibility in the financing strategy.

The 2008 financial crisis and more recently the COVID-19 crisis have demonstrated that financial markets can become illiquid suddenly and/or for an extended period, even in advanced economies. In the event of financial stress, market participants can be hesitant to lend to the government, especially when they perceive a higher risk with respect to the sovereign's financial position. In such cases, the government may prefer to revise borrowing plans rather than locking in very high interest rates that may result from financial contagion or a temporary spike in risk aversion (Guscina, Malik and Papaioannou, 2017[5])). In an extreme scenario, a confluence of global and domestic factors might result in a complete loss of market access, which, in turn, could trigger capital flight and exacerbate exchange rate pressures, even for governments with limited budget deficits (e.g. Iceland before the 2008-09 financial crisis). In view of these considerations, sovereign borrowers often build flexibility through contingency funding plans, such as establishing credit line(s) with commercial banks, cash advances with central banks, maintaining a liquidity buffer (i.e. minimum level of cash balance) and, increasing issuance of short-term debt from money markets (e.g. Treasury Bills, and repos). In addition, keeping continuous communication with the investors and transparency prove to be a valuable tool for increasing financial flexibility, as well as enhancing market confidence.

Liquidity buffer practice:

The speed of the DMO's ability to react to market developments and to adapt borrowing plans is an important component of prudent debt management. Revisions to borrowing plans such as timing, size and instrument of issuance require a certain timeframe for the decision-making as well as market communication. A sufficiently large liquidity buffer can help a government to meet its immediate financing needs within the span of this reaction time, thereby safeguarding a sovereign's ability to meet obligations in situations where normal access to funding markets may be disrupted or delayed.

Keeping a certain amount of cash helps governments to avoid temporary shortfalls in cash balances and cope with volatile cash flows. A liquidity buffer enables quick access to liquidity and supports government cash managers in their roles by ensuring that a sufficient amount of liquidity is available when it is needed and at the lowest fiscal cost (Hurcan, Koc and Balibek, 2020[6]) when compared with prevailing market costs. Depending on how a liquidity buffer is funded, however, there may be a cost of carry for having this precautionary tool.

Several OECD countries — including Denmark, Hungary, Mexico and Poland — adapted their CB policies in the aftermath of the 2008 financial crisis (Cruz and Koc, 2018[7]). The objective was to boost market confidence in the government's financial capacity and to provide more flexibility in funding options in the event of stressed market conditions. Country experiences during the European debt crisis highlighted the importance of having a cushion against periods of heightened sovereign stress, as well as against the potential loss of market access. Greece, Iceland, Ireland, and Portugal, have reviewed their CB policies to increase the level of balances to boost market confidence in a government's financial capacity. For example, in Iceland the government's domestic buffer target was set at ISK 120 billion (around 6% of GDP) in 2010, sufficient to meet the largest payments due and to service debt for almost one year (OECD, 2019[8]). In the following years, the target level was lowered as the country regained full access to the market.

The 2020 survey of the OECD Working Party on Debt Management (WPDM) on primary market developments reveals that a few DMOs, noting the benefit of keeping a cash buffer during the turmoil in March, have increased the size of cash buffers (e.g. Canada, Portugal and the United States). For example, the US Treasury adopted a cash buffer policy in 2015 to protect against a potential loss of market access for auctions, and decided to increase its cash balance to USD 800 billion in 2020 in view of larger size and greater uncertainty of cash outflows. It was with the same prudent risk management perspective that the Austrian Treasury adopted a cash buffer policy for the first time in March 2020, in the face of the COVID-19 pandemic. In the case of Portugal, a cash buffer policy was adopted in 2012 and from 2014 onwards a target of 30% to 40% of the gross funding needs of the following 12 months has been followed. During the early months of the health crisis, given the interest rates spike and volatility jump, the cash excess was depleted and only replenished in May once market stability was restored. Compared with the year before, cash reserves increased and risked exceeding the top end of the target range in December 2020. In 2020Q4, the budget outturn and the disbursement of EU funds to support COVID-19 employment protection schemes surprised on the upside at a time the issuance programme was already too advanced to accommodate the unanticipated downward revision of the funding needs.

Diversification in source of funding:

Diversification of funding sources reduces reliance on any one group of investors, which in turn limits potential volatility in markets. Having a diversified funding base (e.g. domestic investors, foreign investors, retail investors and institutional investors) could provide key strategic advantages in dealing with refinancing risk, in particular for countries where borrowing needs have increased substantially and are expected to remain high in medium to long-term. While the investor base of a government debt portfolio is predominantly a result of market forces, a variety of instruments and a range of maturities can be used to build a broad investor base as well as reaching out to new investor groups (OECD, 2019[8]). In particular, countries with substantial refinancing needs may benefit from increasing the appeal of government securities to different investor groups.

Designing and using longer-term instruments to lengthen the nominal yield curve that would match investor preferences is an important strategic consideration. Introducing new securities with long-term maturities would not only help mitigate refinancing risks in the medium and long-term, but also generate additional demand from available domestic and international savings pools (OECD, 2020[9]). For example, in the United Kingdom, long-dated conventional and indexed-linked bond programmes (e.g. 40-year maturities), supported by structural demand from the United Kingdom pension and insurance sectors have helped to increase average duration of issuance and to mitigate refinancing risk since 1980s. The weighted average term-to-maturity has been increased from 14 years in 2007 to almost 18 years in 2019.

During 2020, several sovereign borrowers introduced new securities, as funding needs of governments have increased substantially. The US Treasury introduced 20-year maturity bond in early 2020, which received strong demand from long-term investors such as pension funds. New securities such as green bonds might also help reaching out climate sensitive investors and institutional investors with long-term investment horizon. Maturity of sovereign green bonds issued so far have varied from 5 to 30 years, with a weighted average maturity of 18-years.

Establishing credit lines:

Establishing credit lines with commercial banks, or a short-term cash advance facility from central banks can also help to build flexibility. For example, following the COVID-19 shock, the Bank of England has temporarily extended the use of the government's 'Ways and Means (W&M) facility' to manage liquidity and the short-term volatility of cash forecasts. Thus far, the United Kingdom debt management office has not used this facility.

Similarly, establishing swap lines with central banks can help ease currency pressures, and mitigate refinancing risk of foreign debt. Following the pandemic, several countries signed or enhanced existing bilateral swap arrangements with major central banks (e.g. Australia, Brazil, Japan, Malaysia, Mexico, Korea, Singapore and Thailand).

Access to liquid money markets:

Money markets are often, but not necessarily, the most liquid segment of financial markets, and money market instruments (e.g. Treasury bills and commercial papers) can offer flexible and relatively cheap financing conditions for a short time. Normally, issuance of short-dated securities lowers average maturity of debt issuance and elevates refinancing risk. However, when facing significant uncertainty concerning funding conditions, or funding needs, sovereigns, –particularly those with high credit ratings– can potentially benefit from issuing in money markets to generate flexibility in funding operations, and meet emergency funding and any temporary cash shortfalls at low costs. Given that this strategy also entails high refinancing risk, sovereign issuers should balance the use of money market instruments over time, and when they better understand how permanent the increase in funding needs is, they replace them with long-term debt.

Sovereign debt managers assess T-bills as 'shock absorbers'. It is because T-Bill markets, often the most liquid segment of the yield curve, enables sovereign issuers to manage uncertainties regarding financing requirement in the most cost-effective way (For further information, see Chapter 1, Box 1.1. Issuance of T-Bills to navigate shocks). During the 2008 financial crisis, the share of short-term debt issuance of OECD governments in gross issuance climbed to over 55%. In the years following the crisis, T-bill issuance moderated and the share of short-term debt issuance declined to below 40% of gross issuance in 2019. Sovereign issuers followed a similar strategy to address large unexpected financing needs due to the COVID-19 shock. In 2020, majority of pandemic-related debt was issued in the form of T-Bills in the US, France, Germany and Japan with almost no cost (e.g. 6 month Treasury bill yields negative in the euro area, Japan and 0.1% in the United States).

Role of transparency and communication in times of stress:

A sovereign debt management office's ability to finance governments can be adversely affected by exogenous changes in economic and market conditions. Anticipating and mitigating potential impacts of changes in these conditions requires continuous monitoring and communication. Sovereign DMOs should maintain regular contact with primary dealers as well as end-investors. This is not to supervise the market, but to help gather market intelligence and develop an understanding of the investor base and its prevailing concerns, as well as potential demand for various borrowing instruments. In particular, with refinancing needs of most sovereigns having increased substantially, it is prudent to consider demand from various buy-side and sell-side participants of government securities markets when reviewing the volume of instruments and auction sizes.

Furthermore, at times when market sentiment deteriorates to the point that sustaining market access is at stake, a concentrated focus on investor engagement plays a critical role in managing refinancing risk. Experiences of the 2008 financial crisis and the subsequent European sovereign debt crisis suggest that having an investor relations programme is an effective tool for developing long-term relationships with investors, broadening the investor base, and providing transparency on the macroeconomic situation and funding plans (OECD, 2019[8]).

Improving the transparency of refinancing risk is likely to reduce investor uncertainty, leading to more credible debt management and lower borrowing costs (OECD, 2016). Disclosure of key indicators as well as liquidity buffer policies help to improve confidence between investors and sovereigns. Therefore, DMOs should try to include this information as part of their communication tools (e.g. annual reports, monthly bulletins and investor presentations).

Enhanced transparency of strategies, operations and policies for public debt management reduces investor uncertainty, thereby increasing the appeal of government bond markets. This in turn broadens the investor base, lowers risk premiums and eases borrowing costs (OECD, 2016[10]). The role of transparency and communication becomes even more important in stressed periods. The 2020 survey of the OECD Working Party on Debt Management (WPDM) on secondary market developments indicates that DMOs have regularly updated investors through email distribution lists, press releases, publishing market notices on their websites regarding changes in funding needs and plans in response to the COVID-19 crisis. While the pandemic restrained travel and face-to-face meetings, communication with investors has been to a large extent carried out via conference calls (including videoconferencing). In addition, in some countries, senior government officials have played a larger role in communicating changes in funding needs and information on programs and operations (e.g. Australia, Canada, the United Kingdom, and the United States). In addition, Primary Dealers have been directly and more frequently contacted in order to reinforce their significant role in helping to manage the huge increase in debt issuance, and efficiency of government securities markets.

The level of uncertainty associated with expenditure on COVID-19 and its impact on the economy has hindered most countries' ability to estimate financing requirements for the whole financial year of 2020. Several DMOs have taken a cautious approach in communicating the uncertainty around the new funding needs as well as the revisions to refinancing strategies, in particular at the initial stage of the crisis during March and April 2020. For example, German debt agency, "Finanzagentur" announced an update of its quarterly issuance plan in April 2020 following its first press release in March 2020 (German Finanzagentur, 2020[11]) (German Finanzagentur, 2020[12]). A cautious approach was taken in terms of highlighting potential changes associated with financing requirements and auction calendar linked to fiscal measures and market conditions. At the same time, providing timely information with comprehensive explanations has helped to manage investor expectations and ease uncertainty.

References

Arellano, C. and A. Ramanarayanan (2012), "Default and the Maturity Structure in Sovereign Bonds", *Journal of Political Economy*, Vol. vol. 120/no. 2, pp. pp. 187–232, http://www.jstor.org/stable/10.1086/666589. Accessed 23 Feb. 2021. [2]

Arslanalp, S. and T. Tsuda (2014), "Tracking Global Demand for Advanced Economy Sovereign Debt", *IMF Working Paper*, Vol. WP/12/284, https://www.imf.org/external/pubs/ft/wp/2012/wp12284.pdf. [4]

Blommestein, H., M. Elmadag and J. Ejsing (2012), "Buyback and Exchange Operations: Policies, Procedures and Practices among OECD Public Debt Managers", *OECD Working Papers on Sovereign Borrowing and Public Debt Management*, Vol. No. 5, https://doi.org/10.1787/22264132. [13]

Cole, H. and T. Kehoe (2000), "Self-Fulfilling Debt Crises", *The Review of Economic Studies,*, Vol. vol. 67/no. 1, pp. pp. 91–116, http://www.jstor.org/stable/2567030. Accessed 23 Feb. 2021. [1]

Cruz, P. and F. Koc (2018), "The liquidity buffer practices of public debt managers in OECD countries", *OECD Working Papers on Sovereign Borrowing and Public Debt Management, No.9*, https://doi.org/10.1787/3b468966-en. [7]

German Finanzagentur (2020), "Issues planned by the Federal government in the second quarter of 2020", *Press release*, Vol. April, https://www.deutsche-finanzagentur.de/fileadmin/user_upload/pressemeldungen/en/2020/2020-03-23_pm01_EK_Q2_en.pdf. [12]

German Finanzagentur (2020), "Issues planned by the Federal Government in the second quarter of 2020 and reopening of outstanding Federal bonds", *Press release* 1, https://www.deutsche-finanzagentur.de/fileadmin/user_upload/pressemeldungen/en/2020/2020-04-07_pm02_Emissionsplanung_en.pdf. [11]

Guscina, A., A. Malik and M. Papaioannou (2017), "Assessing Loss of Market Access: Conceptual and Operational Issues", *Working Paper*, Vol. 17/246, https://www.imf.org/en/Publications/WP/Issues/2017/11/15/Assessing. [5]

Hurcan, Y., F. Koc and E. Balibek (2020), "How to Set Up A Cash Buffer: A Practical Guide to Developing and Implementing a Cash Buffer Policy", *IMF How-To Note No. 2020/004*, https://www.imf.org/en/Publications/Fiscal-Affairs-Department-How-To-Notes/Issues/2020/12/21/How-to-Set-Up-A-Cash-Buffer-A-Practical-Guide-to-Developing-and-Implementing-a-Cash-Buffer-49955. [6]

International Monetary Fund. Strategy, Policy, & Review Department (2021), "Review of the debt sustainability framework", *IMF Policy paper*, Vol. No. 2021/003, https://www.imf.org/en/Publications/Policy-Papers/Issues/2021/02/03/Review-of-The-Debt-Sustainability-Framework-For-Market-Access-Countries-50060. [14]

Jonasson, T. and M. Papaioannou (2018), "A Primer on Managing Sovereign Debt-Portfolio Risks", *IMF Working Paper*, Vol. 18/74, https://www.imf.org/en/Publications/WP/Issues/2018/04/06/A-Primer-on-Managing-Sovereign-Debt-Portfolio-Risks-45746. [3]

OECD (2020), "Sovereign Borrowing Outlook", https://doi.org/10.1787/dc0b6ada-en. [9]

OECD (2019), *OECD Sovereign Borrowing Outlook 2019*, OECD Publishing, Paris, https://dx.doi.org/10.1787/aa7aad38-en. [8]

OECD (2016), *OECD Sovereign Borrowing Outlook 2016*, OECD Publishing, Paris, https://dx.doi.org/10.1787/sov_b_outlk-2016-en. [10]

Notes

[1] IMF defines public debt sustainability as follows: "In general terms, public debt can be regarded as sustainable when the primary balance needed to at least stabilize debt under both the baseline and realistic shock scenarios is economically and politically feasible, such that the level of debt is consistent with an acceptably low rollover risk and with preserving potential growth at a satisfactory level" (International Monetary Fund. Strategy, Policy, & Review Department, 2021[14]).

[2] Countries that can issue domestic currency debt generally face much lower refinancing risk, particularly for very short-term (t-bills) that are accepted as collateral by the domestic central bank. In the OECD area, governments predominantly finance their budget deficits through local currency denominated debt. For example, local currency share of total central government marketable debt in the OECD area is about 95 percent as of 2020.

[3] Credit rating agencies also consider the share of non-resident as an assessment criterion. For example, Standard&Poors sees a risk factor if non-residents hold consistently more than 60% of government marketable debt.

[4] Life and non-life insurance companies hold 19.5% of outstanding Japanese Government bonds as of December 2020; the insurance companies and pension funds hold around 28% of outstanding Gilt issuance in the United Kingdom as of as of September 2020.

[5] For instance, the central bank holds around 45% of outstanding national central government bonds in Japan and Sweden, above 20% in Germany, the United Kingdom and the United States (as of December 2020).

[6] Average Time to Re-fixing (ATR) is a measure of weighted average time until the principal payments in a debt portfolio become subject to a new interest rate. A low (high) ratio indicates that the interest rates of the debt portfolio re-set in a short (long) period and therefore increases (decreases) the risk. Further discussion on this indicator is available in the 2016 edition of the Sovereign Borrowing Outlook.

[7] Bond switches and buybacks are also used to increase the issuance of on-the-run securities above and beyond what would otherwise have been possible. The resulting more rapid build-up of new bonds enhances market liquidity of these securities. (Blommestein, Elmadag and Ejsing, 2012[13])

3 The impact of the COVID-19 crisis on emerging market borrowing

In the global fight against the COVID-19 pandemic and its detrimental social and economic impact, governments have launched various measures since March 2020. This, combined with reduced tax revenues, has resulted in an upsurge in sovereign borrowing needs globally. While most advanced economies have been experiencing ultra-low interest rates and strong demand for public debt, a number of underlying vulnerabilities have made borrowing conditions more difficult for many developing and emerging market economies.

The pandemic greatly complicated the ability of developing and emerging market sovereign issuers' to access to the markets in 2020, in particular at the initial stages of the crisis. The global risk-off environment resulted in sharp reversal of capital flows, which had a particularly profound impact on market access of non-investment grade issuers. This chapter presents an overview of debt issuance trends in developing and emerging market economies, and assesses the impact of the COVID-19 crisis on issuance conditions.

3.1. Introduction

In 2020, this publication explored sovereign debt issuance developments in developing and emerging markets and developing economies (hereafter 'EMEs') for the first time. Chapter 2 of the 2020 OECD Sovereign Borrowing Outlook presented an overview of issuance trends in emerging-market government securities from 2000 to 2019, and touched upon the initial impact of the COVID-19 crisis. The main objective of this second chapter on EMEs is to provide an update on the impact of the COVID-19 crisis on sovereign debt issuance by different income levels and geographic regions, with a particular focus on maturity and currency structure.

The key source of information is a unique n exclusive dataset comprising 10 621 sovereign government securities issued by 88 EME sovereign issuers in 2020 (see Annex for details of the methodology used).

Key findings

- The COVID-19 shock initially caused sharp fluctuations in capital flows to EMEs, leading to deterioration in sovereign funding conditions, particularly for CCC and lower graded sovereign issuers. Following rapid responses by central banks, funding conditions eased relatively rapidly in the second half of the year, but remained fragile.

- A number of EME sovereign issuers were downgraded in the wake of the pandemic as a result of strained budget conditions and weak economic outlook. Thirty countries, the majority of which were associated with the non-investment grade, experienced 68 downgrades in 2020.

- In total, EME sovereigns issued about USD 3.4 trillion of debt in financial markets in 2020. Compared to the average of the previous five years, the amount issued was 35% higher, but was driven by fewer issuers in 2020. Overall sovereign funding costs, which had surged dramatically during the initial phase of the Covid-19 pandemic, fell down close to pre-pandemic levels towards the end of the review period amid an environment of ample global liquidity.

- While emerging Asia, led by People's Republic of China (China), continued to be the largest emerging regional issuer in 2020, issuance by other regions including MENA and Sub-Saharan Africa were below the historical averages.

- The impact of global risk aversion was much more pronounced on market access of low- and lower middle-income countries compared to other EMEs during 2020. The result was a sharp decline in net debt issuance relative to previous 5-year averages.

- Another important impact of the lower appetite for EMEs sovereign debt throughout 2020 was the decline in the share of foreign currency-denominated debt issuance in total debt issuance, with the exception of euro. The decline was particularly marked in the MENA and Sub-Saharan African regions, where foreign currency borrowing was most costly.

- Maturity of borrowings shortened dramatically at the initial stages of the crisis across EMEs. As market conditions improved, investment-grade issuers were able to increase the share of long-term securities. Again, the impact was larger for non-investment grade issuers, where T-Bills accounted for 45% of total borrowing in 2020.

- In view of global risk factors that could put strong downward pressure on EME sovereign borrowing conditions, greater attention to refinancing risk of EME sovereign debt is warranted. Countries that have access to market funding may benefit from lengthening debt maturities and build-up contingency buffers through pre-financing programmes. Countries with limited or no market access will continue to require official sector grants and loans to ease their financing constraints, and in some cases, debt relief.

3.2. The pandemic has weighed greatly on emerging market sovereign issuers

In the wake of the COVID-19 crisis, governments of many EMEs have faced two sources of intense funding pressures: financing needs arising from the COVID-19-related measures, and refinancing of the outstanding debt at unreasonable interest costs. The impact of the crisis on EME sovereign funding varied widely in terms of the social and economic consequences of the epidemic, the country's capacity to use fiscal policy to mitigate these consequences, including their stage of development and efficiency of local currency bond markets.

While many EMEs entered the COVID-19 crisis with public debt already at elevated levels, the pandemic weighed considerably on investor risk appetite, and exposed pre-existing vulnerabilities in these economies (OECD, 2020[1]). The circumstances were particularly challenging for countries with less fiscal leeway, limited policy buffers and constrained market access. Despite the challenging market conditions with episodes of high volatility, EMEs survived 2020 without experiencing a materialisation of the systemic debt crisis, largely due to the global monetary and fiscal policy response to the crisis, as well as rapidly arriving good news on vaccination development and debt relief by the international community.

3.2.1. Funding conditions have improved, but vulnerability to global risk sentiment remains high

In EMEs, funding conditions are vulnerable to global risk sentiment and therefore historically more volatile than in advanced economies (e.g. fears of contagion of the European sovereign debt crisis to EMEs in 2011, the 'taper tantrum' in 2013, political tensions between the United States and China as well as monetary policy tightening in the United States in 2018). At the onset of the COVID-19 crisis, a sharp deterioration in investor sentiment and risk appetite translated into a sudden reversal of capital flows. The cost of EM sovereign borrowing surged dramatically in March and April 2020, due to sharp increases in EM risk premiums (Figure 3.1). This, in turn, particularly affected the financing ability of countries that lack deep and liquid local currency bond markets.[1]

Figure 3.1. Spreads on EM sovereign debt

Panel A: Evolution between January 2010 and February 2021
Panel B: Evolution between January 2020 and February 2021

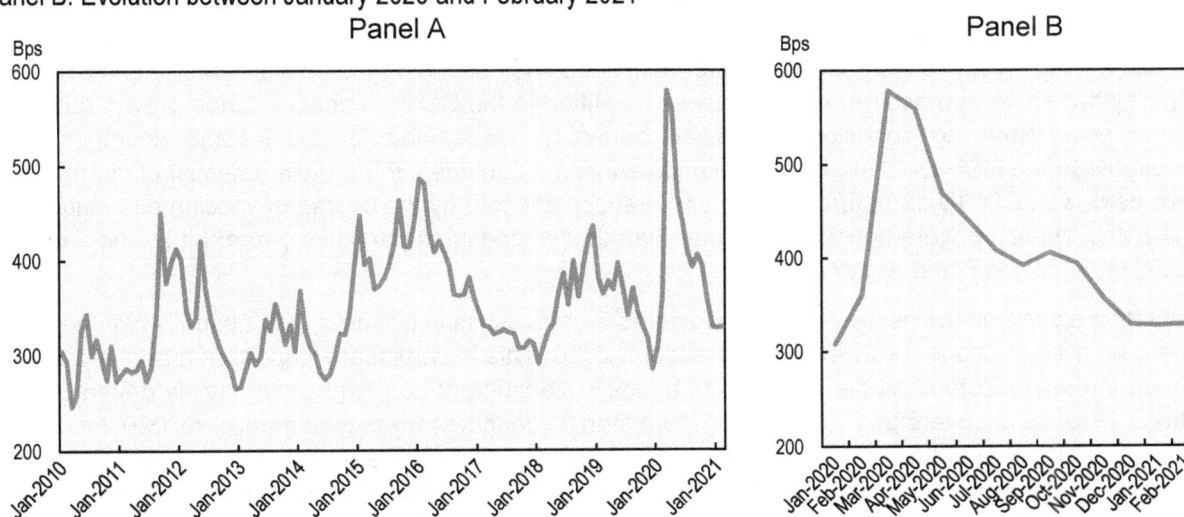

Notes: JP Morgan Emerging Markets Bond Indices. Y axes are cropped to help show changes between dates.
Source: Factset.

While yields across all the EM sovereign bond categories have deteriorated, "CCC and lower rated sovereign bonds in particular were affected more strongly (Figure 3.2). This resulted in a wide differential between high-yield and investment-grade bonds, which in turn impaired some countries' access to international capital markets when it was needed the most.

Figure 3.2. Yields on external EM government securities

Panel A: Yield group evolution between January 2020 and January 2021

Panel B: Changes in yield for CCC and lower rated securities on a month on month basis (2020)

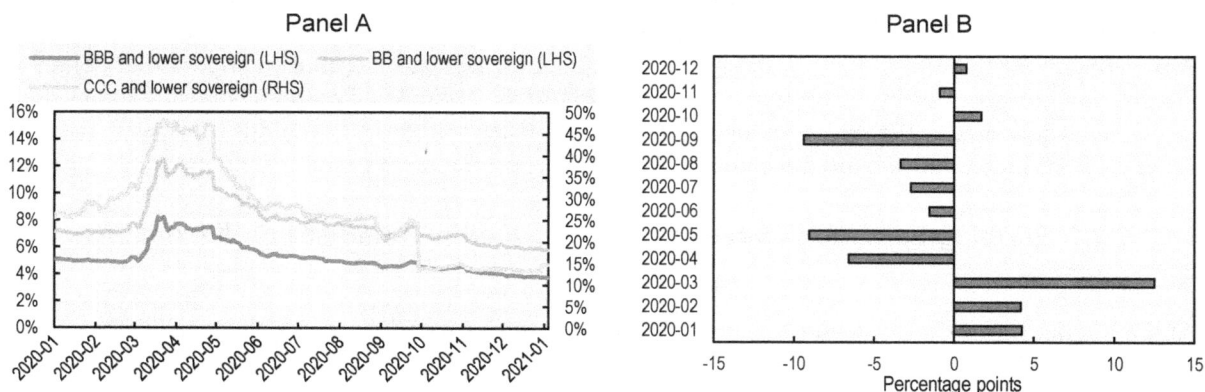

Source: Bank of America ICE EM Indices, Refinitiv and OECD calculations.

Following the initial shock of the pandemic, the stress in financial markets eased rapidly, largely due to the massive and unprecedented scale of actions by major central banks, in particular the Federal Reserve and the ECB. Several large EM economies also eased their monetary policy stance. For example, several central banks have bought local currency government bonds to fight the effects of COVID-19, including Colombia, Indonesia, Mexico, Poland, South Africa, Turkey and the Philippines (Cantú et al., 2021[2]). In addition to central banks' commitment to support market functioning, the global wave of fiscal stimulus and positive developments with regard to vaccines have helped improve the global growth outlook. Towards the end of 2020, yield spreads compressed significantly across EMEs, and fell down close to pre-pandemic levels. As investor risk sentiment improved, demand for emerging market sovereign bonds picked up. At the same time, investors increasingly differentiated countries based on their policy stability and availability of policy buffers to address market volatilities in addition to the COVID impact on their growth outlook. In this respect, financing conditions remained generally constrained for low-income countries (LICs) vulnerable to the COVID-19 shock. Within middle-income countries, the growth potential of countries that have dealt with COVID-19 outbreaks well and are less affected by the course of vaccine distribution (e.g. China and Thailand) were considered higher than that of countries particularly hard hit by the virus (e.g. Brazil, India, Mexico, and South Africa).

Reflecting a surge in the perceived risk associated with investing in EM debt, an unusually high number of emerging market economies were downgraded in 2020. This is particularly important for sovereigns that rely on foreign investors, as the inclusion of bonds in benchmark bond indices is mainly driven by credit ratings. In terms of sovereign credit ratings, more than 30 countries were downgraded in 2020, the majority of which took place in the initial stage of the crisis. In total, there were 68 downgrades, more than 50% higher than in the most recent spikes of 2016 and 2017 (Figure 3.3).[2] The downgrades largely stemmed from the worsened macroeconomic outlook, amid the pandemic. It is important to note that the majority of credit rating changes have occurred in the non-investment category in the wake of the COVID-19 crisis, leaving several middle-income countries including Angola, Belize and Zambia deeper into highly speculative territory.

Figure 3.3. Changes in EM sovereign credit ratings

Panel A: Number of ratings changes in each year between 2000 and 2020

Panel B: Number of ratings changes in each month of 2020

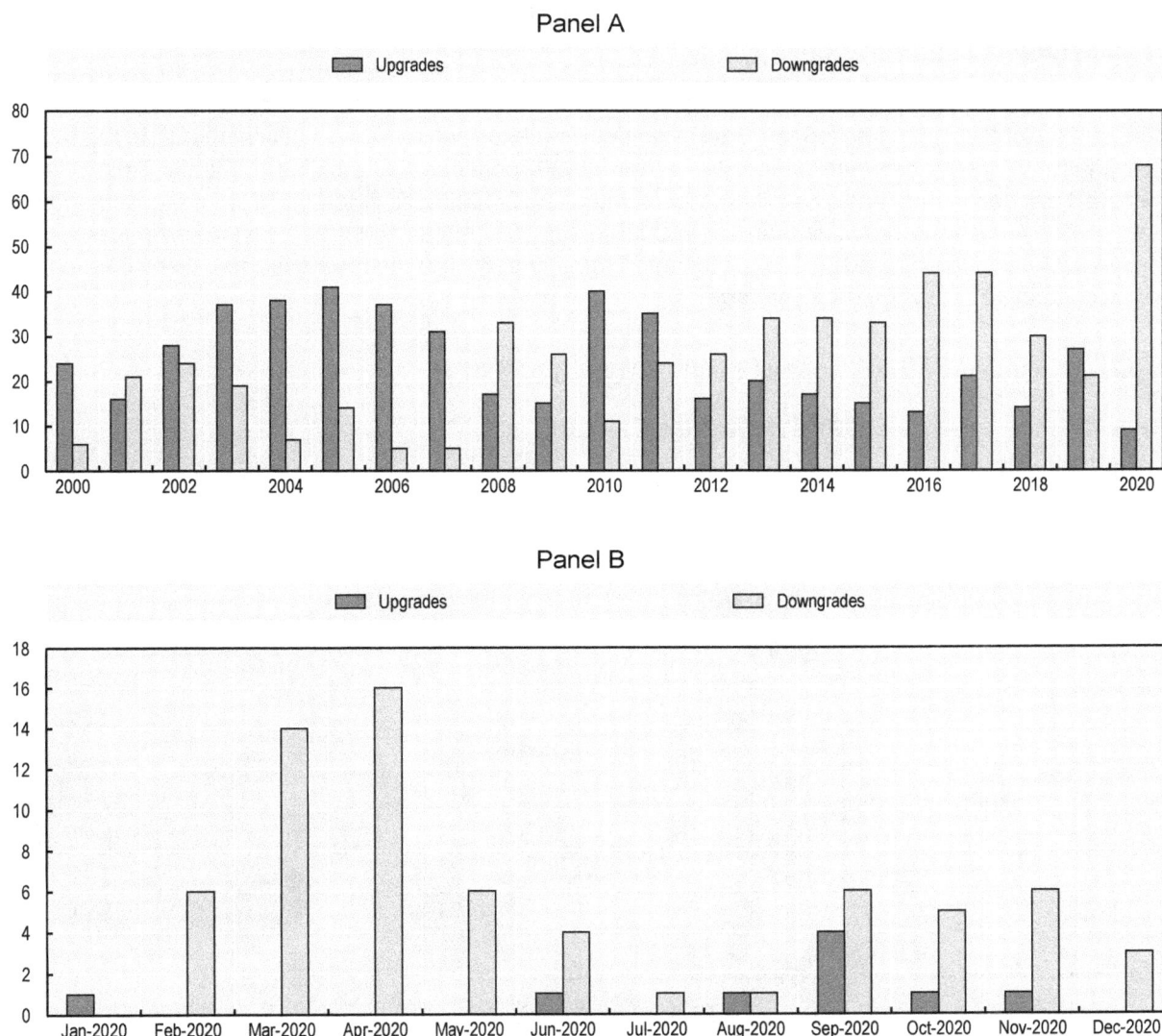

Panel A

Panel B

Notes: Above ratings are based on Moody's, S&P and Fitch and observed on a monthly basis. Aa change in rating by one agency is counted as 1 in the above chart, meaning that if all three agencies change their ratings in one month, it is counted as 3. When there is more than one change per agency in a month, the lower rating has been chosen, except in the case where the lowest rating is a default rating.
Source: OECD calculations based on data from Refinitiv.

While sovereign issuers survived the initial shock, they are still exposed to global risks that could trigger a sudden change in investor sentiment. A particular risk stemming from rising US interest rates could trigger a reversal of capital flows and sharp currency depreciations, as experienced during the "taper tantrum" of 2013. This could pose a significant challenge especially to middle- and low-income countries with large external financing needs and high debt levels. In this regard, stronger-than-expected inflation due to US fiscal stimulus would also heighten such risks (OECD, 2021[3]). While the dependence of most EM economies on external financing is currently lower than in 2013, other factors such as the continued weakness of international travel and tourism, as well as rising commodity prices may put pressure on the external balances of commodity exporters and tourism-based economies. This environment makes EM debt yields more sensitive to global interest rate fluctuations, and amplifies refinancing risk for vulnerable borrowers.

3.2.2. Debt issuance has picked up, though remained lower than historical averages in some regions

Sovereign funding needs of EMEs soared as a result of simultaneously declining fiscal revenues and increasing fiscal stimulus packages.[3] Sovereign debt issuance, which was slightly higher than the average of the last five years between January and April 2020, continued to pick up gradually amid relatively improved risk sentiments after the initial stage of the COVID-19 shock. In total, EM sovereigns raised more than USD 3.4 trillion in financial markets in 2020, over 35% higher than the previous five-year average (Figure 3.4). Investment-grade issuers accounted for almost 70% of the total issuance, up by 8 percentage points compared to the historical average.

Figure 3.4. Gross central government debt issuance by EMEs

Panel A: Monthly issuance in 2020, and average of 2015-2019

Panel B: Issuance in 2020 by investment grade category

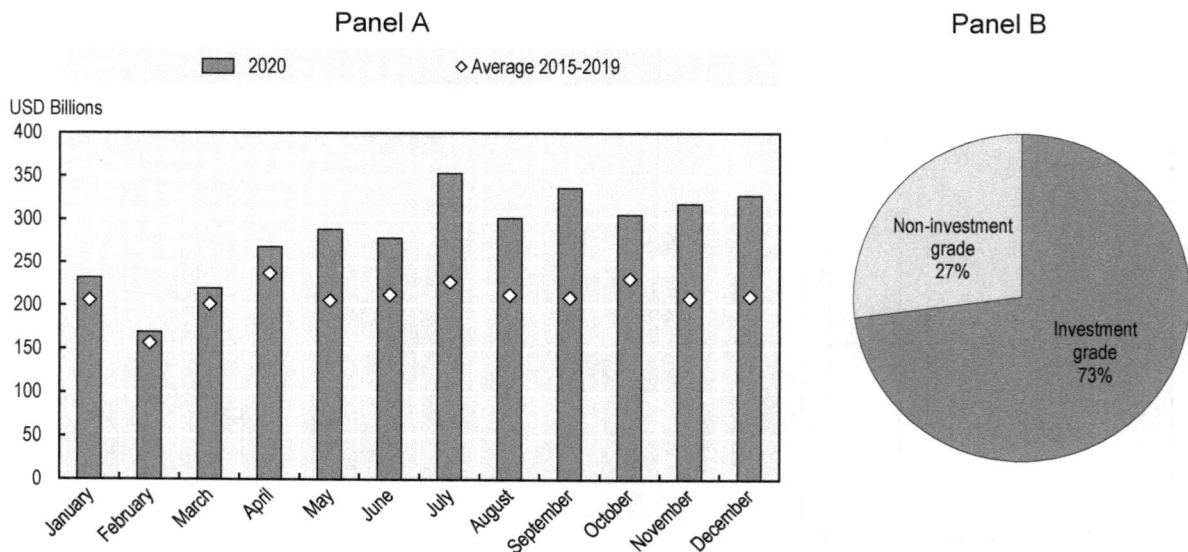

Source: OECD calculations based on data from Refinitiv.

Emerging Asia remained the largest regional issuer, while many other regions lagged behind historical averages

As discussed in the 2020 edition of this publication, the regional composition of EM debt issuance had changed significantly over the preceding decade. In particular, as Emerging Asia became the largest regional issuer, the relative size of debt issuance by the Latin America and the Caribbean, MENA and Sub-

Saharan Africa regions reduced significantly (OECD, 2020[1]).[4] The COVID-19 crisis has only strengthened these patters. In 2020, Emerging Asia remained the largest regional emerging market issuer, accounting for more than 50% of the total issuance (Figure 3.5 Panel A). Even excluding China, issuance capacity of the Emerging Asia region has recovered well from the COVID-19 shock, and debt issuance exceeded the previous five-year average. Most countries in this region have weathered the pandemic relatively well, supported by sound macroeconomic fundamentals, developed local-currency bond markets, as well as timely and effective public health measures (OECD, 2021[3]). Similarly, emerging countries in Europe including Hungary, Poland and Romania significantly increased their borrowings from the market largely due to increased government spending to address the economic consequences of the COVID-19 crisis on businesses and households.

Market-based financing remained constrained for some countries with weak fundamentals. In terms of share of debt issuance, Latin America and the Caribbean, MENA and Sub-Saharan Africa regions fell short of the historical averages (Figure 3.5 Panel A). In particular the Sub-Saharan Africa region, where debt issuance in markets was increasing from very low levels in the pre-pandemic period, was affected most by the crisis. As discussed in the following sections, access to international markets has weakened for many African countries, causing not only the amount of borrowing from the market to decrease, but also the shortening of the maturities.

Figure 3.5. EM sovereign debt gross issuance by regional and income categories

Panel A: Regional composition of debt issuance

Panel B: Issuance by selected income categories

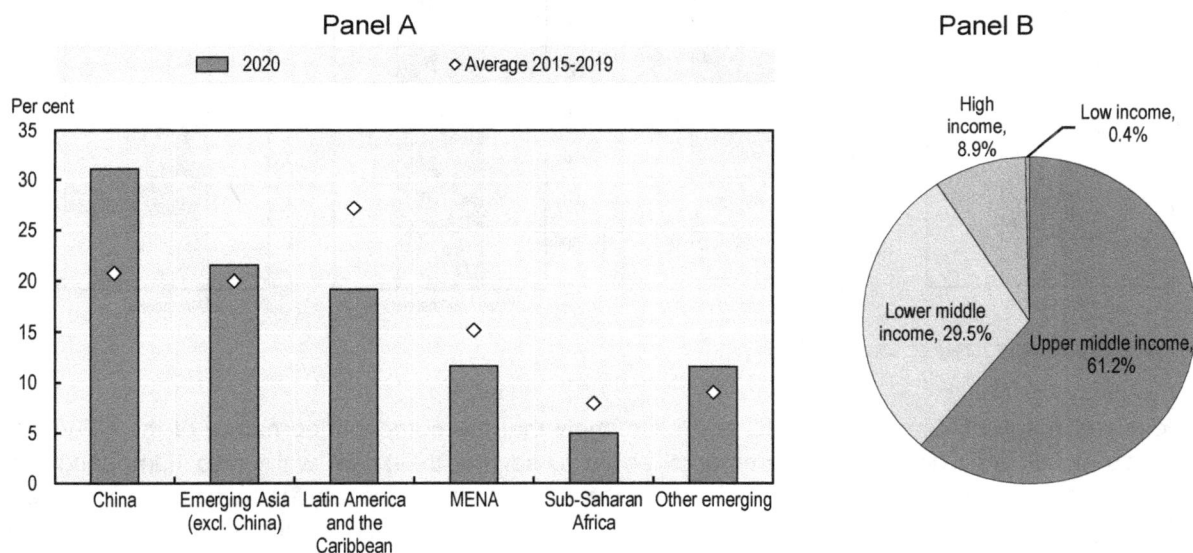

Source: OECD calculations based on data from Refinitiv.

Upper-middle-income countries maintained an upward trend despite the pandemic, thanks to accommodative monetary policies

In 2020, upper-middle-income countries (UMICs) who would have high financing needs and developed institutional frameworks, represent the majority of the total debt issuance according to the income criterion (Figure 3.5 Panel B). The ability to finance budget deficits at reasonable cost and desirable maturities requires, above all, a well-functioning, stable and liquid local currency bond market. A majority of middle-income countries meet their financing needs from the markets with regular issuance programmes. As demand for EM sovereign debt recovered from the initial impact of the COVID-19 shock in the second half of the 2020, debt offerings from middle-income countries have enjoyed strong demand, which allowed them to issue new debt to finance increased fiscal spending and to refinance existing debt (Figure 3.6). The LMICs and the LICs, on the other hand, have decreased their new borrowing. Furthermore, net debt issuance by LICs was even negative for a few months of 2020. This means that they were unable to rollover some of their scheduled debt repayments, let alone raise new borrowing in the markets. These countries with shallow domestic debt markets or, constrained market access, are often more vulnerable to changes in market conditions than other EM countries. Consequently, during 2020, they relied heavily on aid, grants and concessional financing from multilateral institutions.

Figure 3.6. Net debt issuance by selected income categories (billions USD)

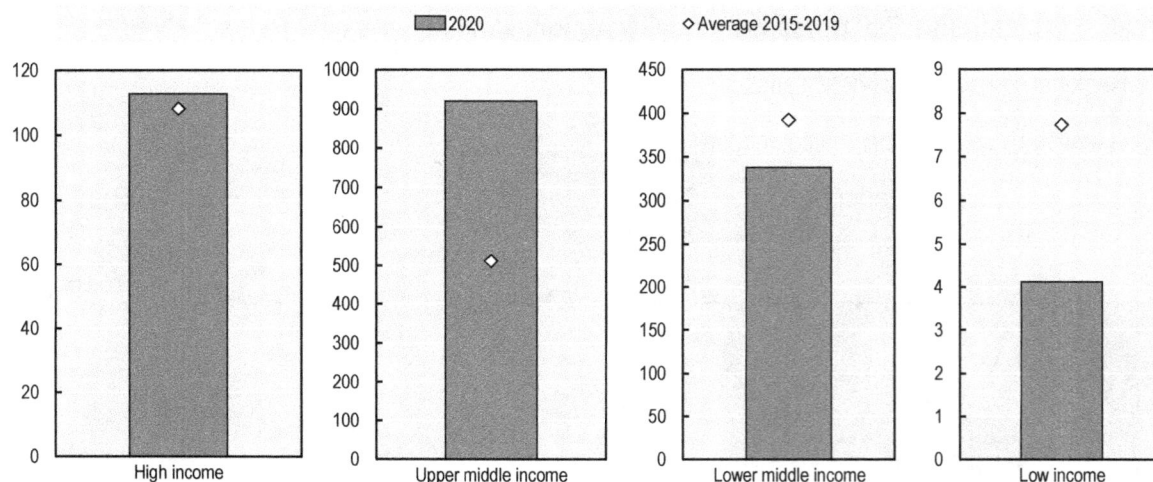

Source: OECD calculations based on data from Refinitiv.

Low levels of net debt issuance in LMIC and LICs imply that the compounded nature of the COVID-19 shock has significantly damaged governments' ability to service their debt while also hampering their response to the pandemic and their ability of making the investments necessary for the economic recovery. The fiscal situation has been particularly dire in these economies, where the impact of COVID-19 has aggravated pre-existing high debt levels and hampered local currency bond markets. The international financial community's efforts through various facilities have helped to ease these countries' liquidity constraints and prevented a potential debt crisis since the onset of the COVID-19 crisis (Box 3.1). Although significant efforts have been made in this direction, the international community has recently highlighted the need for more support in light of the uncertain global outlook (OECD, 2021[4]). Particularly, the possibility of disorderly rise in bond yields in the advanced economies, and especially in the United States, may put pressure on funding costs in EMEs.

Box 3.1. International efforts to support debt resilience and improve debt transparency

In April 2020, the G20 nations offered to suspend debt service payments owed by 73 low- and lower-middle income countries, and invited private creditors to follow the suit. The Debt Service Suspension Initiative (DSSI) is for a limited period (initially from May to December 2020, then extended until the end of 2021 following the meeting of Central Bank Governors and Finance Ministers in April 2021). As of February 2021, more than 60% of the eligible countries have requested debt service suspensions, while about USD 5 billion worth of debt service was suspended in 2020. This facility primarily aims to address immediate liquidity needs, but not debt sustainability problems.

When debt is unsustainable, an orderly debt restructuring is often the most viable solution for both borrowers and investors. Debt restructuring can help to limit market disruption and spillovers. With these considerations in mind as well as the need for deeper debt relief in some cases, the G20 and Paris Club countries agreed on a Common Framework for Debt Treatments in November 2020. This framework takes a case-by-case approach applied to the countries eligible for the DSSI, excluding middle-income countries. In practice, only a few countries (e.g. Chad, Ethiopia, and Zambia) have applied for debt treatment under this framework, largely due to the uncertainties linked to its implementation, fears of losing hard-earned market access, and of potential ratings downgrades. At the same time, the International Monetary Fund (IMF) provided financial assistance and debt service relief to numerous countries with its USD 1 trillion lending capacity.

These measures created some breathing space for the countries that were able to benefit from them in 2020. Despite these concerted efforts, daunting development challenges remain. In 2021, more support from the multilateral organizations and private creditors will be needed not only for low-income countries, but also for middle-income countries. Hence, the IMF has recently proposed a new Special Drawing Rights allocation of USD 650 billion to provide additional liquidity to the global economic system. In addition, G20 bilateral official creditors agreed to a final extension of the DSSI through end-December 2021. Further policy actions which have been considered are: i) adjustment of the common framework to broaden eligible countries; ii) raising ODA commitments and optimizing Multilateral Development Banks' concessional financing.

Against this backdrop, the OECD supports improving the liquidity and resilience of public debt for solvent but vulnerable countries; streamlining debt restructuring processes when necessary; and across all borrowing countries, improving debt management capacity and transparency. Called upon by the G20, and with the support of the UK government, the OECD has recently launched a Debt Transparency Initiative to collect, analyse, and report on debt levels of low-income countries in alignment with the Institute of International Finance's (IIF) Voluntary Principles on Debt Transparency. This initiative brings together multilateral institutions, central banks, finance ministries, civil society organisations, and commercial banks through an Advisory Board for Debt Transparency, which will be established under the Committee on financial Markets. The project aims to shed new light on previously opaque bilateral lending to low-income countries by providing stakeholders with more comprehensive and accurate public debt data.

Source: IMF COVID-19 Financial Assistance and Debt Service Relief, Remarks by Angel Gurría, Secretary-General at High-Level Meeting with Heads of State and Government on the International Debt Architecture and Liquidity on March 29, 2021, The Bretton Woods Committee report titled 'Sovereign Debt: A Critical Challenge', and OECD Debt Transparency Initiative.

3.3. Currency and maturity structure varied widely among country groups

The maturity and currency composition of debt portfolio matters in terms of potential exposures to market and refinancing risks. A portfolio with long average maturity and a low share of foreign currency-denominated debt can help minimise the magnitude of external and domestic shocks on the sovereign borrower.

In view of the importance of having a deep local currency bond market, some emerging economies have developed sophisticated capital markets and were able to issue most of their debt in domestic currency before the pandemic. On average, domestic currency issuance by EM sovereigns accounted for 90% of total issuance between 2000 and 2019, which varied significantly between countries, largely depending on the state and functioning of local currency bond markets (OECD, 2020[1]). In particular, local currency share of borrowing has increased substantially in Emerging Asia, where sudden reversals of capital flows have depressed sovereign balance sheets facing currency mismatch and caused several debt crises in the past.

Maturity of borrowing is mainly determined by market forces in EMEs. Investors' tolerance for risk, long-term financial objectives and market liquidity determine the cost of borrowing at different maturities, and so the trade-off between cost and risk of different borrowing strategies. During the period from 2000 to 2019, EM investment-grade sovereign issuers managed to lengthen the average maturity of their issuance to over eight years; while the average maturity of non-investment grade borrowing declined from 5.8 to 4.5 years over the same period (OECD, 2020[1]).

In some cases, market demand for longer-term maturities may be insufficient, unstable, or offering too costly terms. As discussed in Chapter 2, strong and sustainable demand from institutional investors such as insurance companies and pension funds that tend to have long-term investment horizons enables sovereigns to issue longer-dated bonds on a regular basis. This is the case for advanced economies (e.g. Germany, Japan, France and the UK). However, for many EMEs, with low domestic savings and few institutional investors, the capacity to issue long-term debt in local currency bond markets is limited, even in normal times. In this regard, bond issuance in international markets with relatively longer maturities allows EM sovereigns to reduce their exposure to rollover and interest rate risk and diversify their investor base. On the other hand, heavy reliance on external funding can increase country's exposure to 'sudden stops' in international capital markets. The COVID-19 crisis has greatly affected currency and maturity structure of EM sovereign debt, in particular for issuers with underdeveloped local currency bond markets and weak fundamentals.

3.3.1. T-Bill issuance by non-investment grade issuers has increased

Given the uncertainty about future spending needs and the severe liquidity problems faced by sovereign issuers, many EM governments have turned to money markets to raise funds to meet their current obligations and to build a cushion for future economic shocks. Affected by swings in investor sentiment, market demand for long-term instruments became less stable and more costly for emerging market and developing economies in 2020. As a result, the prevalence of shorter-term T-Bill issuance has increased. In March 2020, at a time of acute market distress, the share of local currency T-Bills surged dramatically, accounting more than 60% of total issuance by both investment and non-investment grade categories. In the following months, however, issuance by investment grade countries, benefiting from benign financing conditions, has shifted towards longer-term bonds. On average, T-Bills accounted for 34% of the total issuance by investment grade issuers between May and December 2020. For non-investment grade issuers, the ratio stands around 45% on average, noticeably elevated around the US election and the second wave of Covid-19 built up.

Figure 3.7. Maturity composition of debt issuance by investment and non-investment grade categories in 2020

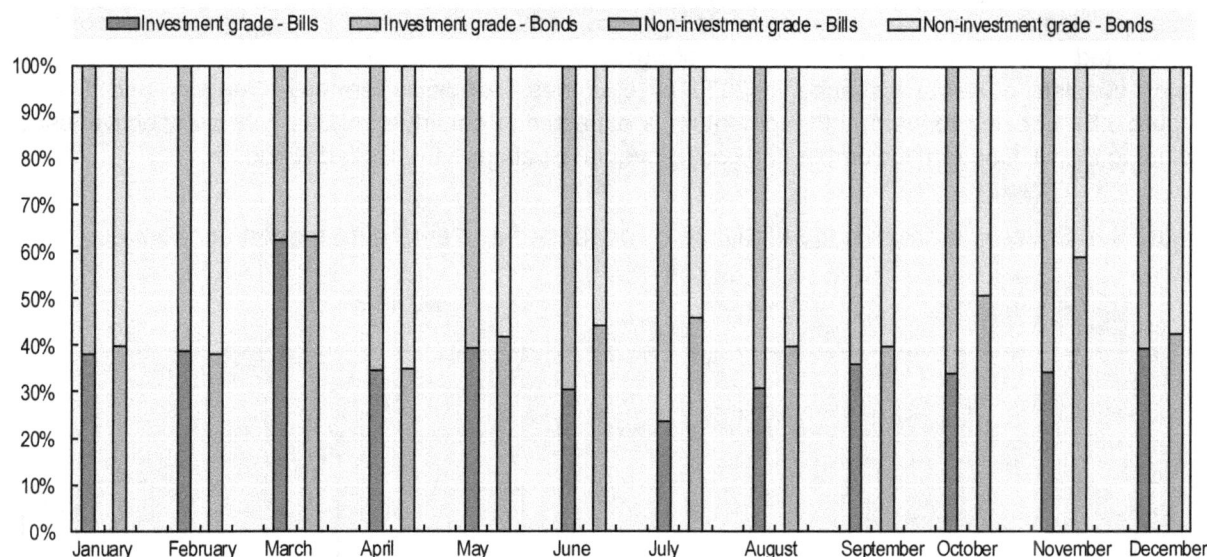

Source: OECD calculations based on data from Refinitiv.

3.3.2. The pandemic is spurring the issuance of new instruments

In order to support raising funds to face the current COVID-19 crisis and to diversify their investor base, several EM sovereigns have introduced new instruments such as saving bonds, social bonds, infrastructure bonds and green bonds (e.g. Ecuador, Egypt, Hungary, Mexico, and Thailand). Depending on their maturity and currency structure, new instruments can be useful to moderate the exchange rate, interest rate and rollover risks of debt portfolios. Often, saving bonds, attracting domestic retail investors, are issued in local currency with long-dated maturities. Social bonds, infrastructure bonds and sovereign green bonds, to finance projects with different objectives, also carry long maturities (from 5 to 30 years). In terms of the currency choice, EM sovereigns often issue these bonds in international capital markets in USD to attract a broader investor class.

In addition, the issuance of social, green infrastructure and other green bonds helps achieve the climate goals set at the Paris Agreement and the SDG goals related to infrastructure, poverty and climate challenges. Of particular interest is the acceleration in green bond issuance by EM governments to meet long-term climate and infrastructure targets in recent years (Box 3.2). As of March 2021, total issuance of green bonds by EM governments reached USD 11 billion, more than half of which has been issued since 2020.

Box 3.2. Sovereign green bond issuance accelerated in 2020, helping to promote green growth

Among the alternative investment products tailored to low carbon transition that have emerged, green bonds have been preferred by sovereign issuers as well as environmentally conscious investors. They feature broader benefits to the financial market by promoting the development of a domestic market for green bonds, and enabling market participants with different investment horizons to find a green, transparent, high-quality investment opportunity at their disposal.

Sovereign green bond issuance has exceeded USD 130 billion globally since Poland and France kicked off four years ago. Amid the rising imminence of sustainability issues, such as the climate change, increased borrowing needs due to the COVID-19 pandemic have widened the scope for green bond issuance. Hence, sovereign green bond issuance by both advanced and emerging market economies accelerated in 2020, which helped to promote green growth. 40% of the outstanding sovereign green bonds consists of debut issuance in 2020 by countries including Germany, Hungary and Thailand (Figure 3.8). Looking forward, this momentum is expected to continue in 2021 with prospective issuers including Brazil, Canada, Colombia, Mexico, Slovenia, Spain and the United Kingdom.

Figure 3.8. Sovereign green bond issuance by advanced and emerging market economies

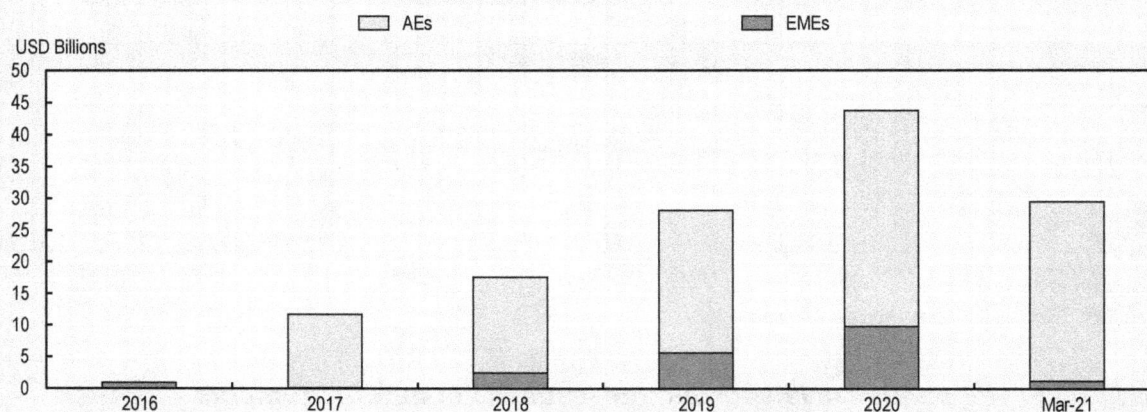

Source: Refinitiv, national authorities' websites and OECD calculations.

In terms of maturity structure and size, sovereign green bonds vary significantly: Maturity of bonds varies from 5 to 30 years, with a weighted average maturity of 18-years, and size of bond issues (including re-openings) ranges from USD 15 million to above USD 30 billion. While euro area issuers account for around 75% of outstanding sovereign green bonds, the number of EM issuers is growing fast. Hence, the share of total annual issuance by EMEs increased to 23% in 2020.

Issuing a green bond entails specific features

Green bond issuance entails specific requirements in terms of coordinating the various line ministries responsible for extracting project information required for monitoring and reporting purposes as well as special marketing and reporting exercises. These idiosyncratic requirements can deter many EMEs with limited resources and limited capacity from issuing green bonds. In addition, it might prove challenging for many small EMEs lacking investment grade to appeal international investors, in particular institutional investors, despite the fact that an issuer can have the bond and framework rated by a specialised research provider or rating agency.

In view of challenges with regard to the issuing process and the capacity gap, potential EM issuers may benefit from other countries' experiences as well as international financial organisations such as the World Bank Group in terms of preparing the policy framework, leveraging media interest, market intelligence and project screening (International Finance Corporation, 2018[5]). Fiji, for example, benefited from the World Bank Group in preparation and implementation of the policy framework in 2017. Similarly, Nigeria whose sovereign green bond was rated "GB1", the highest possible rating by Moody's, received support from international bodies like the IFC (International Finance Corporation) and the UN Environment Programme (UNEP).

3.3.3. Domestic currency securities continue to dominate EM issuance, while some issuers faced challenges in regaining access to international markets

Overall, domestic currency securities continued to dominate EM issuance in 2020, suggesting deepening of local currency bond markets and an improvement in currency risk exposures in EMEs. On average, domestic currency issuance accounted for 92% of total issuance by EMEs in 2020, slightly higher than historical averages. At the regional level, in Emerging Asia, where local currency bond markets have become relatively developed in recent years, domestic currency debt issuance constituted 97% of total issuance in 2020. The ratio is lower in emerging countries in Europe, as a number of EU countries that are not in the euro area including Bulgaria, Croatia, Hungary, Poland and Romania benefit from access to euro markets.

Overall, FX-denominated issuance varied widely among EMEs in 2020. While high-grade issuers returned to the market rapidly from April 2020 onward, issuers with weak fundamentals faced significant challenges in regaining market access after the initial months of the crisis. In a few countries including Turkey, FX-denominated debt issuance in domestic markets increased significantly.[5] FX-denominated issuance in Sub-Saharan African and MENA countries (where foreign currency financing increased notably before the pandemic), was particularly weak, reflecting a loss of international market access (Figure 3.9). Between March and October 2020, there was no FX-denominated issuance from Sub-Saharan African countries.

Middle-income issuers with established track records of good economic performance and positive medium-term outlook continued to tap the international capital markets in 2020. The largest issuers were investment-grade issuers, including Mexico, Poland, Saudi Arabia and Qatar. Of particular interest is that China, for the first time, issued USD- and euro-denominated bonds in international capital markets and Peru sold USD-denominated 'century bonds' to soften the economic fallout from the coronavirus crisis. In addition to investment-grade issuers, several non-investment grade issuers including Albania, Belarus, Jordan, El Salvador and Ukraine, issued debt in international capital markets. It is important to note that a handful of LMICs, including Benin, Honduras, Mongolia and Uzbekistan, which are classified as income-eligible for the G20 Debt Service Suspension Initiative, issued Eurobonds post-COVID-19.

Figure 3.9. Foreign currency denominated debt issuance within emerging market groups

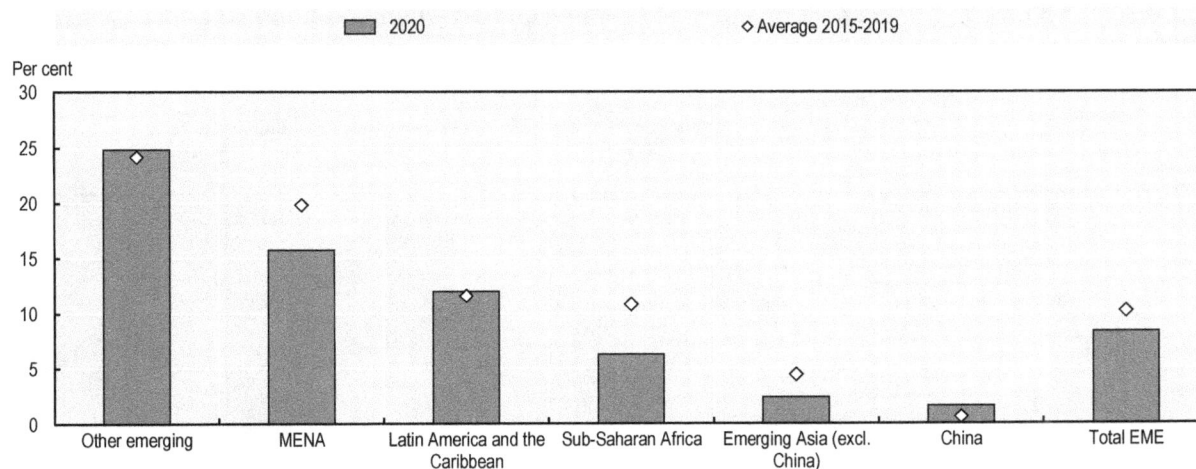

Source: OECD calculations based on data from Refinitiv.

In addition, a few countries with already elevated debt levels, including Argentina and Ecuador, conducted debt restructuring operations in the second half of 2020. These recent examples of debt restructuring have shown that Collective Action Clauses can help facilitate renegotiation with bondholders, and in turn, an orderly restructuring process (Ian and Dimitrios, 2021[6]).

3.3.4. USD remained the most popular foreign currency of debt issuance

Compared to the historical averages, the share of USD- and Japanese yen-denominated issuance in total FX-denominated debt issuance declined in 2020 (Figure 3.10). By contrast, the share of euro-denominated bond issuance increased on the back of increased issuance by emerging countries of Europe, including Romania, Poland, Hungary and Serbia. Nevertheless, USD-denominated issuance, accounting for more than 70% of total FX-denominated debt issuance, remained the most popular foreign currency for international debt issuance by EME sovereigns in 2020.

Figure 3.10. Composition of foreign currency denominated debt issuance

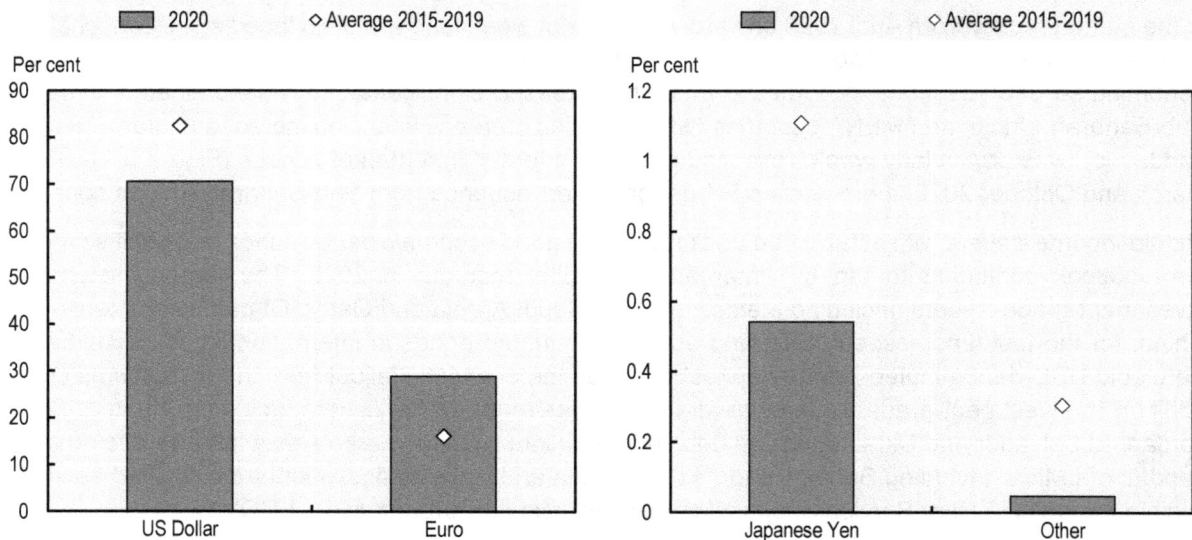

Source: OECD calculations based on data from Refinitiv.

Figure 3.11. Volume share by yield group of fixed-rate USD denominated bond issuance by EMEs in 2020

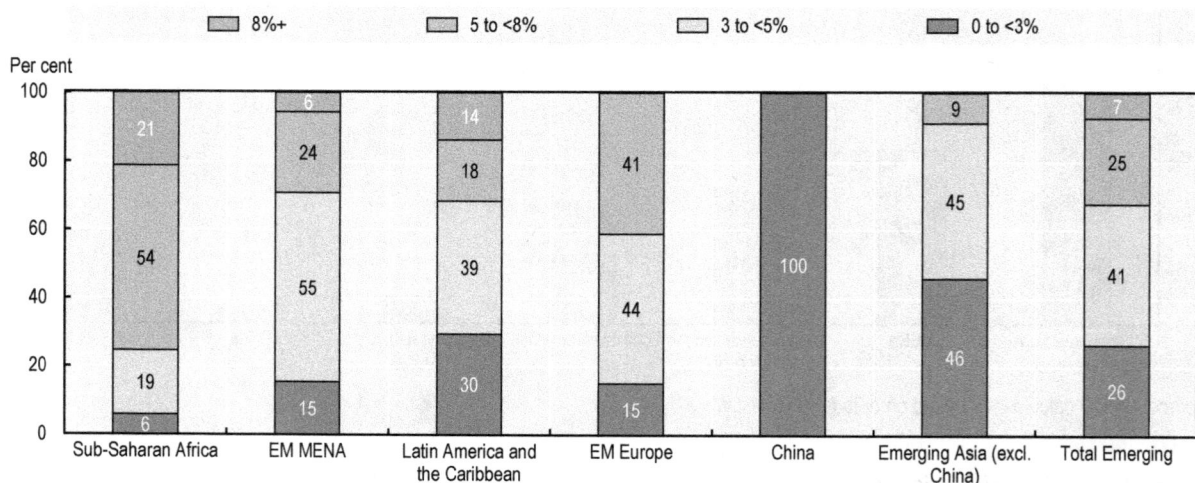

Source: OECD calculations based on data from Refinitiv.

The volume share by yield group of fixed-rate USD denominated bond issuance has also shown variation among regions in 2020 (Figure 3.11). About one quarter of the total fixed-rate USD-denominated government bonds were issued with less than 3% yield in 2020; 41% between 3 and 5% yield, and 32% with more than 5% yield in the primary market. Looking at regional groups, the cost of USD-denominated bonds was relatively favourable for Emerging Asia issuers. Emerging Africa, on the other hand, issued USD denominated debt with the highest average costs as reliance on commodities, tourism and remittances has made some of these countries' finances particularly vulnerable to the COVID-19 shock (e.g. Angola for oil prices, Seychelles for tourism) (IMF, 2021[7]). In this region, three quarters of total USD debt was issued with higher than 5% yield, one third of which was even higher than 8%.

3.4. Increased financing and shorter maturities amplified medium-term refinancing needs

The COVID-19 crisis has increased government debt to be repaid by EMEs, largely due to increased borrowings to finance various measures to mitigate the social and economic impacts of the pandemic. In addition, the average maturity of issuance by EMEs shortened from 7 years in 2019 to 6.4 years in 2020. Average maturities shortened more drastically in some countries where the COVID-19 virus hit hard. For example, in Brazil, federal debt held by the public due within the next 12 months increased from 18% in December 2019 to above 28% in December 2020.

Higher rollover risk is reflected in increasing rollover ratios for the coming years. 15% of outstanding EME government securities is due in 2021, and 21% within the subsequent two years (Figure 3.12). Of particular interest is that the impact on maturities was more pronounced in countries where foreign holdings of domestic debt declined sharply as in many cases non-resident investors favour the longer maturity spectrum during risk-off episodes. For example, in Indonesia, the share of 10-year bonds in outstanding government debt declined from 39.2% in 2019 to 35.1% in 2020, as the share of foreign holdings fell from 38.6% to 25.2% during the same period.[6] Similarly, in Thailand, where the share of foreign holdings decreased from about 17% in 2019 to 13.6% in 2020, debt due within three years has increased by USD 19.6 billion (equal to 10% of total government debt) over the same period.

Figure 3.12. Outstanding government debt due within the next 3 years (by selected income groups)

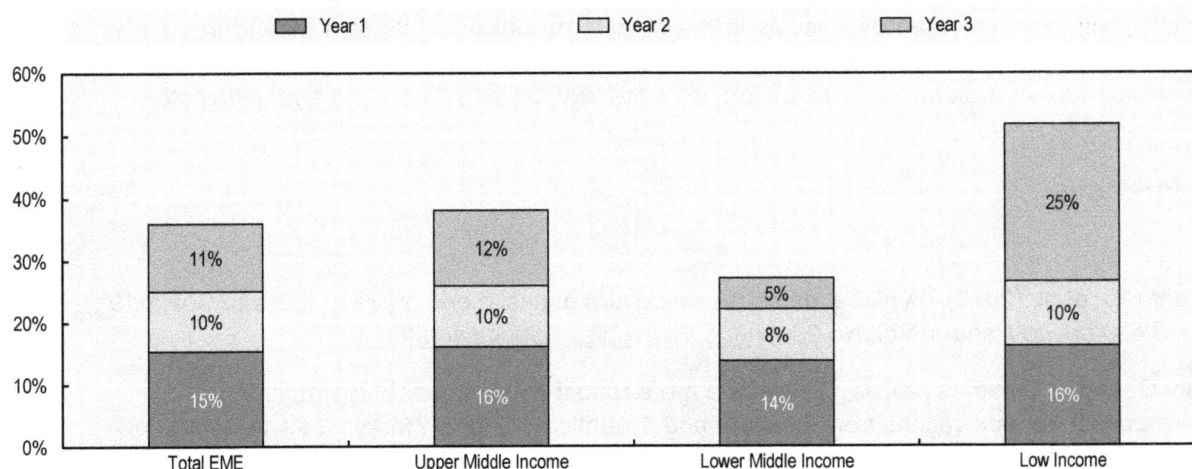

Source: OECD calculations based on data from Refinitiv.

Compared to middle-income countries, refinancing needs are much higher in LICs where debt due in the next three years was 51% in 2020. Higher near-term debt repayments imply a higher refinancing risk and pass-through impact of interest rate changes on government interest costs, which in turn would further increase borrowing needs and tighten overall domestic financial conditions.

3.4.1. Emerging market issuers should be vigilant amid continued global uncertainty

Credit ratings downgrades and rising debt levels on the back of higher refinancing needs amid the pandemic have not translated into consistently high funding costs for EM sovereigns, largely due to ultra-accommodative monetary policies deployed by major advanced economies. In total, EM sovereigns issued about USD 3.4 trillion of debt in financial markets in 2020, 35% higher than the average of previous five years. Additionally, increased borrowing in shortened maturities has raised financing pressure in the near future.

Looking forward, a number of risk factors could put strong downward pressure on EM sovereign funding conditions including rising inflation expectations and weak economic recoveries due to slower distribution of vaccines, and renewed waves or new variants of the COVID-19 virus. Such potential risk scenarios call for greater attention to refinancing risks in EMEs. A particular risk for EMEs is that rising US bond yields could trigger a reversal of capital flows and higher currency volatility, similar to the 'taper tantrum' of 2013. A re-evaluation of inflation risks in the context of large monetary and fiscal support, or earlier-than-expected withdrawal of policy support in advanced economies would heighten such risks. In particular, countries with high external financing needs and high near-term rollover ratios are more susceptible to changes in the market sentiment.

In view of the still-high risk tolerance in global financial markets, a prudent means of managing public debt would require lengthening of maturities to limit short-term refinancing risk and limit potential future issuance volatility. In addition, these countries may benefit from building-up contingency buffers through pre-financing programmes.

LICs with weak fundamentals, on the other hand, are the most vulnerable to global risks, as they have a relatively low level of reserves and with limited financial buffers and other contingency safety nets. In addition, LICs' external financing needs are expected to increase. The average annual amount of external debt service falling due in 2021-25 is more than twice the pre-crisis average (2010-19) (International Monetary Fund. Strategy, Policy, & Review Department, 2021[8]). While market access may remain limited for LICs with very elevated debt levels in the near term, official sector grants and loans such as ODA grants, multilateral credits and lending from IFIs will help ease their financing constraints. In cases where necessary, further debt restructuring might be necessary to avoid disastrous spending cuts.

References

Cantú, C. et al. (2021), "A global database on central banks' monetary responses to Covid-19", *BIS Working Papers*, Vol. No 934, https://www.bis.org/publ/work934.pdf.   [2]

Ian, C. and L. Dimitrios (2021), "Towards a more robust sovereign debt restructuring architecture: innovations from Ecuador and Argentina", *Capital Markets Law Journal*, Vol. 16, Issue 1, pp. 31–44, https://doi.org/10.1093/cmlj/kmaa032.   [6]

IMF (2021), *IMF's policy tracker for COVID-19: Policy Responses to COVID19*, https://www.imf.org/en/Topics/imf-and-covid19/Policy-Responses-to-COVID-19.   [7]

IMF and World Bank (2021), *Guidance Note For Developing Government Local Currency Bond Markets*, https://www.imf.org/en/Publications/analytical-notes/Issues/2021/03/17/Guidance-Note-For-Developing-Government-Local-Currency-Bond-Markets-50256. [9]

International Finance Corporation (2018), "Guidance for Sovereign Green Bond Issuers : With Lessons from Fiji's First Emerging Economy Sovereign Green Bond", https://openknowledge.worldbank.org/handle/109. [5]

International Monetary Fund. Strategy, Policy, & Review Department (2021), "Macroeconomic Developments and Prospects In Low-Income Countries—2021", *IMF Policy Paper*, https://www.imf.org/en/Publications/Policy-Papers/Issues/2021/03/30/Macroeconomic-Developments-and-Prospects-In-Low-Income-Countries-2021-50312. [8]

OECD (2021), "OECD Economic Outlook", Vol. Interim Report, http://www.oecd.org/economic-outlook/march-2021/. [3]

OECD (2021), *Remarks by Angel Gurría, Secretary-General*, https://www.oecd.org/about/secretary-general/oecd-sg-remarks-at-international-debt-architecture-and-liquidity-event-29-march-2021.htm. [4]

OECD (2020), "Sovereign Borrowing Outlook", Vol. Special COVID-19 Edition, https://doi.org/10.1787/dc0b6ada-en. [1]

Annex 3.A. Methods and sources

Primary sovereign bond market data and country groupings

Primary sovereign bond market data are based on original OECD calculations using data obtained from Refinitiv that provides international security-level data on new issues of sovereign bonds. The data set covers bonds issued by emerging market sovereigns in the period from 1 January 2015 to 31 December 2020 and includes both short-term and long-term debt. Short-term debt ("bills") is defined as any security with a maturity less than or equal to 367 days. The database provides a detailed set of information for each bond issue, including the proceeds, maturity date, interest rate and interest rate structure.

The definition of emerging markets used in the present report is the IMF's classification of Emerging and Developing Economies used in the World Economic Outlook. The regional definitions are also those used by the IMF, while the income categories used (high income, low income, lower middle income, upper middle income) are defined by the World Bank according to GNI per capita levels.

A number of bonds have been subject to reopening. For these bonds the initial data only provide the total amount (original issuance plus reopening). To retrieve the issuance amount for such reopened bonds, specific data on the outstanding amount on each reopening date for the concerned bonds have been downloaded from Refinitiv. In order to obtain the issuance amount on each relevant date, the outstanding amount on a given date has been subtracted from the outstanding amount on the following date. The reopening data only provide amounts outstanding in local currency. The calculated issuance amounts are converted on the transaction date using USD foreign exchange data from Refinitiv. To ensure consistency and comparability, the same method is used for all bonds, including those which have not been subject to reopening.

Exchange offers and certain bonds in the dataset have been manually excluded when they did not have any identifier (ISIN, RIC or CUSIP) and when they have not been able to be manually confirmed by comparing with official government data.

The issuance amounts are presented in 2020 USD adjusted by US CPI.

Credit ratings data

Refinitiv provides rating information from three leading rating agencies: S&P, Fitch and Moody's. For each country that has rating information in the dataset, a value of 1 to the lowest credit quality rating (C) and 21 to the highest credit quality rating (AAA for S&P and Fitch and Aaa for Moody's) is assigned. There are eleven non-investment grade categories: five from C (C to CCC+); and six from B (B- to BB+). The ratings data are observed on a monthly basis. If a country has received several ratings in one month, the lowest one is used, except when that is a default rating (SD or D for S&P and RD or DDD for Fitch).

The rating in question is then assigned to each relevant bond issued by that country. In the case that there are ratings available from several agencies, their average is used. When differentiating between investment and non-investment grade bonds, if the final rating is higher than or equal to 12 it is classified as investment grade. If the final rating is below 12 but higher than or equal to 11 and at least two agencies have given a rating higher than or equal to 12, it is also classified as investment grade. All other bonds are considered non-investment grade.

Notes

[1] Despite growth in recent years, local currency bond markets which can help absorbing sudden movements in foreign capital flows continue to remain relatively small compared with advanced economies ((IMF and World Bank, 2021[9]).

[2] Several EM countries including Argentina, Costa Rica, Oman and Zambia were downgraded more than twice in 2020.

[3] Compared to advanced economies, support in emerging markets and developing economies has been generally more limited, reflecting limited fiscal space in many of these economies. The demand-supporting spending and revenue measures were much smaller in low-income developing countries (about 2% of GDP on average) than in middle-income emerging market economies (about 6% of GDP) or advanced economies (nearly 24% of GDP) (IMF, 2021[7]).

[4] Emerging Asia region increased its debt issuance share from 19% in 2000 to 44% in 2019 (OECD, 2020[1]). During this period, China nearly tripled its share of total EME debt issuance. Even excluding China, where the debt build-up has been particularly pronounced, debt issuance in Emerging Asia has risen to record highs.

[5] In Turkey, the share of foreign currency denominated debt issuance in total domestic market debt issuance increased from 26% in 2019 to 39.5% in 2020 (Public Debt Management Report, MoF, Turkey).

[6] In Indonesia, despite the decline in the 10-year bonds share in total issuance, ATM of government debt remained high around 8.5 years in 2020, partly because of the Indonesian central bank's purchases of long-term government bonds.

Annex A. OECD 2020 Survey on Primary Markets Developments

This annex belongs to the OECD Sovereign Borrowing Outlook 2021.

Thirty-five of the 37 OECD countries responded to this survey.

Countries which responded to the survey but did not provide comments to a question may not appear in the table of answers.

Source: 2020 Survey on Primary Markets Developments by the OECD Working Party on Debt Management.

Annex A is available ONLINE ONLY at the following DOI:

https://doi.org/10.1787/48828791-en

List of tables in Annex A

Table A.1. Overview of issuing procedures

Table A.2. Q1 Overview of issuing procedures – country notes

Table A.3. Q1b Overview of recent changes in issuing procedures and techniques

Table A.4. Q2 Have you issued or plan to issue any new types of securities like inflation-linked bonds, variable rate notes, green bonds, and longer dated securities?

Table A.5. Q2 New type of instrument that was issued in the LAST 12 months

Table A.6. Q2 New type of instrument that will be issued in the NEXT 12 months

Table A.7. Q2 Other types of securities

Table A.8. Q3 Major challenges experienced over the last 9 months

Table A.9. Q3 Major challenges experienced over the last 9 months – Country notes

Table A.10. Q4 Major risk factors/events faced in the last 12 months

Table A.11. Major risk factors/events which might affect your operations in the next 12 months

Table A.11. Q4 Major risk factors/events which might affect your operations – Country notes

Table A.12. Q5 How these risks are mitigated (e.g. contingency funding plans, continuity plan etc.)?

Table A.14. Q6 Do you consider potential risk factors when preparing your financing plan (e.g. auction calendar)?

Annex B. OECD 2020 Survey on Liquidity in Government Bond Secondary Markets

This annex belongs to the OECD Sovereign Borrowing Outlook 2021.
Thirty-six of the 37 OECD countries responded to this survey.
Countries which responded to the survey but did not provide comments to a question may not appear in the table of answers.
Source: 2020 Survey on Liquidity in Secondary Government Bond Markets by the OECD Working Party on Debt Management.

Annex B is available ONLINE ONLY at the following DOI:
https://doi.org/10.1787/48828791-en

List of tables in Annex B

Table B.1. Domestic currency bond lines

Table B.2. Q2 Do you believe it is necessary/important to maintain certain volumes in specific maturity segments in your country?

Table B.3. What has been the overall trend in the liquidity conditions of your domestic sovereign bonds -in terms of bid-ask spread, trading volumes etc.- over the last 9 months?

Table B.4. Q4 If you answered there was an improvement or a decline in Q3, please specify the main factors that might affect the changes in liquidity conditions?

Table B.5. Q4 If you answered there was an improvement or a decline in Q3, please specify the main factors that might affect the changes in liquidity conditions?

Table B.6. Q4 If you answered there was an improvement or a decline in Q3, please specify the main factors that might affect the changes in liquidity conditions. – Country Notes

Table B.7. Q5 Have you observed changes in liquidity conditions of your foreign bonds over the last 9 months?

Table B.8. Q6 Have you observed changes in liquidity conditions of bond related derivate and repo markets over the last 9 months?

Table B.9. Q7 Do you have measures in place to motivate dealers to provide liquidity?

Table B.10. Q8 Do you undertake any other measures in order to enhance liquidity?

Table B.11. Q8b If yes to Q8, please specify the measures that you undertake to enhance liquidity.

Table B.12. Q8b Other specified measures that you undertake to enhance liquidity measures that you undertake to enhance liquidity

Table B.13. Q9 Have you imposed new requirements on market-makers in their provision of liquidity over the last 9 months?

Table B.14. Q10 If you have adapted your funding strategies and operations in response to the pandemic, how have you communicated the changes in your funding needs and other operations with the market? Please elaborate on the main considerations

www.ingramcontent.com/pod-product-compliance
Lightning Source LLC
Chambersburg PA
CBHW080619270326
41928CB00016B/3129